WORLD HISTORY SERIES ■ ■ ■

Caesar's
Conquest of Gaul

Titles in the World History Series

The Age of Feudalism
The American Frontier
Ancient Greece
The Ancient Near East
Architecture
Aztec Civilization
Caesar's Conquest of Gaul
The Crusades
The Cuban Revolution
The Early Middle Ages
Egypt of the Pharaohs
Elizabethan England
The End of the Cold War
The French and Indian War
The French Revolution
The Glorious Revolution
The Great Depression
Greek and Roman Theater
Hitler's Reich
The Hundred Years' War
The Inquisition
The Italian Renaissance
The Late Middle Ages
The Lewis and Clark Expedition
Modern Japan
The Punic Wars
The Reformation
The Relocation of the North American Indian
The Roman Empire
The Roman Republic
The Russian Revolution
Traditional Africa
Traditional Japan
The Travels of Marco Polo
The Wars of the Roses
Women's Suffrage

WORLD
HISTORY SERIES ■ ■ ■

Caesar's
Conquest of Gaul

by
Don Nardo

Lucent Books, P.O. Box 289011, San Diego, CA 92198-9011

Library of Congress Cataloging-in-Publication Data

Nardo, Don, 1947–
    Caesar's conquest of Gaul / by Don Nardo.
       p. cm.—(World history series)
    Includes bibliographical references and index.
    ISBN 1-56006-301-7
    1. Caesar, Julius—Influence—Juvenile literature. 2. Gaul—
History—Gallic Wars, 58–51 B.C.—Juvenile literature.
3 Great Britain—History—Roman period, 55 B.C.–A.D. 449 —
Juvenile literature.   4. Europe—Civilization—Roman
influences—Juvenile literature.   I. Title. II. Series.
DC62.C2N37   1996
936.4'02—dc20   95-16225
                                        CIP

Copyright 1996 by Lucent Books, Inc., P.O. Box 289011,
San Diego, California 92198-9011

Printed in the U.S.A.

Contents

Foreword

Each year on the first day of school, nearly every history teacher faces the task of explaining why his or her students should study history. One logical answer to this question is that exploring what happened in our past explains how the things we often take for granted—our customs, ideas, and institutions—came to be. As statesman and historian Winston Churchill put it, "Every nation or group of nations has its own tale to tell. Knowledge of the trials and struggles is necessary to all who would comprehend the problems, perils, challenges, and opportunities which confront us today." Thus, a study of history puts modern ideas and institutions in perspective. For example, though the founders of the United States were talented and creative thinkers, they clearly did not invent the concept of democracy. Instead, they adapted some democratic ideas that had originated in ancient Greece and with which the Romans, the British, and others had experimented. An exploration of these cultures, then, reveals their very real connection to us through institutions that continue to shape our daily lives.

Another reason often given for studying history is the idea that lessons exist in the past from which contemporary societies can benefit and learn. This idea, although controversial, has always been an intriguing one for historians. Those that agree that society can benefit from the past often quote philosopher George Santayana's famous statement, "Those who cannot remember the past are condemned to repeat it." Historians who ascribe to Santayana's philosophy believe that, for example, studying the events that led up to the major world wars or other significant historical events would allow society to chart a different and more favorable course in the future.

Just as difficult as convincing students to realize the importance of studying history is the search for useful and interesting supplementary materials that present historical events in a context that can be easily understood. The volumes in Lucent Books' World History Series attempt to present a broad, balanced, and penetrating view of the march of history. Ancient Egypt's important wars and rulers, for example, are presented against the rich and colorful backdrop of Egyptian religious, social, and cultural developments. The series engages the reader by enhancing historical events with these cultural contexts. For example, in *Ancient Greece*, the text covers the role of women in that society. Slavery is discussed in *The Roman Empire*, as well as how slaves earned their freedom. The numerous and varied aspects of everyday life in these and other societies are explored in each volume of the series. Additionally, the series covers the major political, cultural, and philosophical ideas as the torch of civilization is passed from ancient Mesopotamia and Egypt, through Greece, Rome, Medieval Europe, and other world cultures, to the modern day.

The material in the series is formatted in a thorough, precise, and organized manner. Each volume offers the reader a comprehensive and clearly written overview of an important historical event or period. The topic under discussion is placed in a broad historical context. For example, *The Italian Renaissance* begins with a discussion of the High Middle Ages and the loss of central control that allowed certain Italian cities to develop artistically. The book ends by looking forward to the Reformation and interpreting the societal changes that grew out of the Renaissance. Thus, students are not only involved in an historical era, but also enveloped by the events leading up to that era and the events following it.

One important and unique feature in the World History Series is the primary and secondary source quotations that richly supplement each volume. These quotes are useful in a number of ways. First, they allow students access to sources they would not normally be exposed to because of the difficulty and obscurity of the original source. The quotations range from interesting anecdotes to farsighted cultural perspectives and are drawn from historical witnesses both past and present. Second, the quotes demonstrate how and where historians themselves derive their information on the past as they strive to reach a consensus on historical events. Lastly, all of the quotes are footnoted, familiarizing students with the citation process and allowing them to verify quotes and/or look up the original source if the quote piques their interest.

Finally, the books in the World History Series provide a detailed launching point for further research. Each book contains a bibliography specifically geared toward student research. A second, annotated bibliography introduces students to all the sources the author consulted when compiling the book. A chronology of important dates gives students an overview, at a glance, of the topic covered. Where applicable, a glossary of terms is included.

In short, the series is designed not only to acquaint readers with the basics of history, but also to make them aware that their lives are a part of an ongoing human saga. Perhaps they will then come to the same realization as famed historian Arnold Toynbee. In his monumental work, *A Study of History*, he wrote about becoming aware of history flowing through him in a mighty current, and of his own life "welling like a wave in the flow of this vast tide."

Important Dates in the History of
Caesar's Conquest of Gaul

B.C.	2000	1000	600	509	390	265	140	118	100	60	58	5

B.C.
ca. 2000
Tribes of Indo-European nomads migrate from western Asia into Europe

ca. 1000
One group of Indo-Europeans, the Latins, settle the Italian plain of Latium, the future site of Rome

ca. 600
Greek colonists establish the city of Massalia on the southern coast of Gaul, in what is now France; the Greeks and native Gauls begin sporadic trade

ca. 509
A group of well-to-do Roman landowners throw out their king and establish the Roman Republic

390
Migrating Gauls enter northern Italy, defeat the Romans at the Allia River, and sack Rome; after receiving a ransom in Roman gold, the Gauls withdraw to the Po Valley, later known as Cisalpine Gaul

265
Rome completes its unification of all of Italy except for the Po Valley

ca. 140
The Romans control virtually all of the Mediterranean coastal lands

118
The Romans establish the colony of Narbo Martius in southern Gaul and convert the surrounding region into a new province, the Narbonese

100
Gaius Julius Caesar is born into an upper-class Roman family and named for his father

60
To oppose the Senate and gain power, Caesar joins with the wealthy financier Marcus Crassus and popular military general Gnaeus Pompey to form an alliance later called the First Triumvirate; Caesar wins election as consul, one of Rome's two top administrator/generals, for the following year

58
Winter: Caesar assumes proconsulship of the Narbonese; Spring: he attacks and defeats the Helvetii tribe in central Gaul; Autumn: he defeats the Germanic Suebi tribe, led by Ariovistus, near the Rhine River

57
Summer: Caesar gains control of the Belgae, a group of tribes inhabiting northern Gaul; one Belgian tribe, the Nervii, offers fierce resistance; Autumn: he sets up a temporary Gallic administrative structure

56
Spring: Caesar meets with Crassus and Pompey in Cisalpine Gaul to keep the deteriorating triumvirate intact; Autumn: Caesar's naval expert, Decimus Albinus, defeats the Veneti, a tribe inhabiting Gaul's northwest coast, at sea

55

Spring: Caesar stops a migration of Germanic tribes from entering Gaul near the junction of the Rhine and Moselle Rivers; builds a fifteen hundred-foot-long wooden bridge over the Rhine and briefly crosses into German territory to discourage further German border violations; Summer: he leads twenty thousand troops across the English Channel into southern Britain, but a storm wrecks many of his ships, forcing him to call off the invasion

54

Summer: Caesar leads a larger force in a second attempt to invade Britain; Autumn: hampered by the onset of winter and disappointed with minimal gains, he again abandons Britain; rebellious Gallic tribes massacre more than seven thousand Roman soldiers

53

Caesar and his commanders ruthlessly put down the rebels, restoring a semblance of order in Gaul; Crassus dies, and the First Triumvirate falls apart

52

Many Gallic tribes rise in rebellion; Caesar lays siege to the enemy stronghold of Alesia in north-central Gaul, and defeats a huge Gallic army, thereby crushing the rebellion

50

The Roman Senate calls for Caesar to surrender command of his army

49

Caesar defies the Senate and leads his troops across the Rubicon River, in northern Italy, initiating a Roman civil war

48

Caesar delivers Pompey a shattering defeat at Pharsalus in east-central Greece

44

Caesar, now dictator of Rome, is murdered in the Senate on March 15 by a group of disgruntled senators

27

Caesar's grandnephew, Octavian, having won a new round of civil wars, takes the title Caesar Augustus and becomes, in effect, the first emperor of the Roman Empire; Augustus travels to Gaul and announces the formation of three new Gallic provinces: Aquitania, Lugdunensis, and Belgica

A.D.
43

The emperor Claudius orders a successful invasion of Britain, which becomes a new Roman province

ca. 400

Groups of central-Asian nomadic peoples sweep through Europe and into Gaul

ca. 476

Rome's last remnants of power disintegrate, and its former provinces, including Gaul and Britain, fragment into many small, weak, and disorganized kingdoms

The Vista of a New World

On an overcast morning in 52 B.C., the forty-eight-year-old Roman general Gaius Julius Caesar exited his command tent. Clad in a hard leather cuirass, or breast-plate, and a bright red cloth tunic, he dutifully received the salutes of rows of his troops as he strode in front of a sturdy wooden stockade. Eventually Caesar came to a tall siege tower, which was, like the stockade, constructed of freshly felled trees. Finding a ladder, he swiftly climbed to a platform at the tower's summit, where his unit commanders awaited him.

From this elevated vantage the Roman leaders had a clear view of Alesia, the town

they and their army of some fifty thousand soldiers had been besieging for several weeks. Located in north-central Gaul, now France, Alesia was the last remaining stronghold of the most powerful local leader who opposed Caesar's conquest of the region. In the previous six years Caesar had managed to subdue most of the hardy, rustic, tribal peoples the Romans referred to as Gauls. He was confident that his capture of Alesia would cause further Gallic military resistance against the Romans to collapse.

And collapse it did. Caesar's siege of Alesia was successful, although far from

Guided by Roman military engineers, Caesar's troops construct tall siege towers outside of the Gallic fortress of Alesia. The Romans were highly adept in all aspects of the art of siege warfare.

This ancient Roman stone sarcophagus bears a sculptured relief depicting a battle between Roman legionnaires and naked Gallic warriors.

easy, for the Gauls resisted fiercely and bravely. In the following year, using the superior training, weaponry, and supply network of the Roman army, Caesar managed to subdue the last, die-hard Gallic resisters. This marked the end of a long and arduous campaign, one distinguished by tremendous accomplishments, at least from the Roman point of view. In his *Lives of the Twelve Caesars*, the first-century Roman historian Suetonius summed up these achievements, writing:

> During the . . . years of his [Caesar's] command [in Gaul] this is in substance what he did. All that part of Gaul which is bounded by the Pyrenees [mountains at the border of Spain and France], the Alps and the Cervennes [mountains in what is now southeastern France], and by the Rhine and Rhone rivers, a circuit of some 3,200 miles . . . he reduced to the form of a [Roman] province; and imposed upon it a yearly tribute [forced payment of money] of 40,000,000 *sesterces* [standard Roman monetary units]. He was the first Roman to build a bridge and attack the Germans beyond the Rhine, inflicting heavy losses upon them. He invaded the Britons [the inhabitants of Britain] too, a people unknown before, vanquished them, and exacted monies and hostages.[1]

Caesar's years-long campaign in Gaul had important and wide-ranging consequences. First, his Gallic conquests cemented his status as one of the most powerful military and political figures in the Roman world. Leaving the bloody battlefields of Gaul, he went on to challenge his political rivals in a power struggle that shook the foundations of Rome's vast Mediterranean empire.

Even more importantly, however, Caesar's Gallic conquests greatly expanded Roman borders. Rome's dominion now stretched farther north into Europe than ever before and encompassed vast new lands and peoples. "The whole concept and character of the Roman empire had been transformed," writes noted historian Michael Grant in his biography of Caesar. "It was no longer the purely Mediterranean empire which it had been up to now, but an empire of continental and northern Europe as well."[2]

As Rome began to exploit conquered Gaul, the Roman people marveled at the exotic Gallic products that flowed into Italy. Among these were large quantities of gold artifacts, gem-studded shoulder clasps, and jewelry made from amber, garnets, and hard enamels. The strange-looking Gallic weapons, including swords and daggers with beautifully decorated handles, became highly sought-after relics in Rome. No less important were the human products of Gaul. These were the thousands of conquered Gallic tribesmen who now entered Rome as slaves. More significantly, the captured Gallic lands themselves represented a huge new resource for Rome to exploit. As another important Caesar biographer, Ernle Bradford, puts it:

The names of unfamiliar towns and tribes, rivers and immense tracts of land hitherto [before] unknown . . . opened up the vista of a new world to the Roman citizen. Not until, centuries later, Europe discovered America and the Far East would there ever be such a sense of novelty, and of expansion into a realm which seemed to have no limit.[3]

Thus, in a way, by conquering Gaul, Caesar performed the same function for Rome as explorers like Christopher Columbus and Vasco da Gama did for Europe in the 1400s and 1500s. Like the later explorers, Caesar opened up a whole new world that promised to inspire and enrich the old. Sadly, in the process Caesar, in the same manner as his later counterparts, imposed his own ways and values on those he conquered and in so doing obliterated an entire way of life. Paralleling the plight of the native peoples of North and South America, the Gauls had no choice but to give way to conquerors who possessed superior armies. But also like the Native Americans, Caesar's victims put up a valiant fight. Staunchly defending their traditional ways against impossible odds, the Gauls left behind a record of battles, sieges, and savage resistance that has thrilled and fascinated people ever since.

1 An Ancient Kinship Lost: Urban Rome Versus Rural Gaul

Julius Caesar's legendary conquest of Gaul, lasting from 58 to 51 B.C., forever changed the cultural evolution of Europe by fusing the ideas and traditions of two very different societies. The conquest imposed Rome's advanced Mediterranean-based civilization on the less advanced societies that then existed in what the Romans called Transalpine Gaul. This was initially a vaguely defined term describing the areas now occupied by France, Belgium, and western Switzerland. The Romans made a clear distinction between this remote, little-known part of Gaul and the closer, more familiar Cisalpine Gaul, which encompassed the fertile Po Valley, the northernmost region of Italy.

For many centuries before the Roman intrusion into Transalpine Gaul, Gallic civilization there had coexisted with the Greek and Roman cultures to its south along the warm Mediterranean coasts. Like the Romans, the Gauls were mainly farmers. But unlike the Romans, the inhabitants of Gaul lacked the political and military organization for which the Romans became famous. As a result, the development of Gallic civilization slowly but steadily fell behind that of its southern neighbor. While Rome erected great cities, united Italy, and then built a strong Mediterranean empire, the Gauls re-mained largely rural and disunited. In time Rome became increasingly imperialistic, that is, intent on extending its own power and influence over other lands. And the Romans came to see Transalpine Gaul as one more backward but potentially valuable territory that was ripe for the picking.

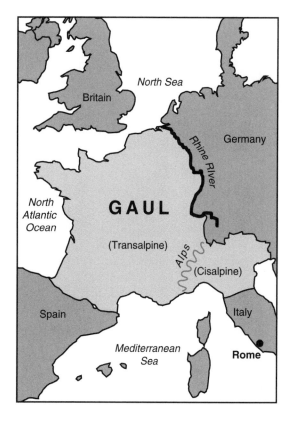

Ancient Migrations

Ironically, the Romans and Gauls, who developed very different modes and levels of civilization, were distantly related. Both were descended from a group of ancient peoples that historians refer to as Indo-Europeans, semicivilized tribal nomads who originally inhabited the vast grassland plains north of the Caspian Sea in western Asia. According to historian James Henry Breasted:

> Divided into numerous tribes, they wandered at will, seeking pasture for their flocks, for they already possessed domestic animals, including cattle and sheep. But chief among their domesticated beasts was the horse. . . . The Indo-Europeans employed the horse not only for riding but also for drawing their wheeled carts. The ox already bore the yoke and drew the plow, for some of the tribes had adopted a settled mode of life, and cultivated grain, especially barley. Being without writing, they possessed but little government and organization.[4]

About 3000 B.C. some of the Indo-European tribes began migrating westward and southward, and by 2000 B.C. they had entered what is now Europe. In the millennium, or thousand years, that followed, some of these peoples remained where they were in eastern and central Europe and adopted a settled, agricultural way of life. Others moved on, turned southward, and populated warm, fertile Mediterranean lands, including Italy. Still others continued westward and settled the areas that later became France, Spain, and Scandinavia. Waves of these nomads even crossed the English Channel and settled Britain. And during all of these long migrations, the various Indo-European waves and groups developed their own individual traits. "As their tribes wandered farther and farther apart," explains Breasted,

> they lost contact with each other. Local peculiarities in speech and customs became more and more marked, finally producing great differences. . . . While at first the Indo-European groups could doubtless understand one another when they met, these differences in speech gradually became so great that the widely scattered tribes, even if they happened to meet, could no longer make themselves understood, and finally they lost all knowledge of their original kinship.[5]

In this way the Latin-speaking group of Indo-Europeans that migrated into north-central Italy shortly before 1000 B.C. lost contact with its cousins in central Europe. The Latins began farming a fertile plain they named Latium, stretching from the western Italian coast inland to the foothills of the Apennine Mountains, which run north-south through the Italian "boot." Meanwhile, other waves of Indo-Europeans, who spoke variations of a language called Celtic, spread through what is now Germany, France, and Britain.

At first these early Latins and Celts were at about the same level of cultural development. They were rustic farmers who raised livestock, lived in crude stone or thatched huts, and used tools and weapons made of stone, copper, and bronze. In time, however, the Latins, under the influence of more advanced Mediterranean peoples—namely the Etruscans and Greeks—began to develop a more organized society. This society de-emphasized tribal differences and united separate local chiefs and leaders under central authorities, usually kings, located in urban centers. The most important Latin urban center was Rome, established perhaps in the tenth century B.C. on a bend in the Tiber River about fifteen miles inland from the western Italian coast. By 600 B.C. Rome had become one of the largest and fastest-growing cities in Italy. The Celts, by contrast, continued to maintain a simpler and far less organized lifestyle. Having no cities or firm central authority, Celtic society remained tribal and rooted in the rural countryside.

Gallic Crafts, Farms, and Trade

But though they were more rural and less politically organized than the Romans, the Celts were far from barbaric and uncivilized, terms the later Romans frequently used to describe the Celtic peoples of Gaul. Celtic tribes and families had a strict and sometimes complex social structure. As in so many other ancient cultures, this structure was dominated by a small upper class of nobles who controlled most of the land. Most members of lower classes, who made up the bulk of the population, lived and worked on the nobles' estates. Some of the larger estates had massive central fortresses called *oppida*. A typical *oppidum* was equipped with strong stone or earthen defensive walls and surrounded by small villages to house the local lord's kinsmen and supporters. The Celts also possessed a

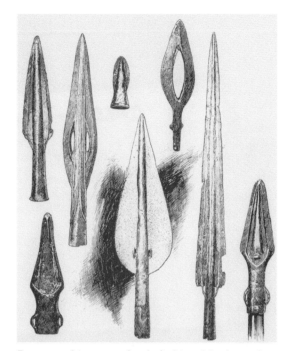

Bronze and iron spearheads fashioned by the ancient Celts who inhabited Gaul.

number of highly developed technical abilities. According to historian Donald R. Dudley, they were

> skilled workers in metals—iron, bronze, and gold. Within the limits of a strict and formal canon [approved style] of art, they could produce superb objects for the luxury trade—brooches, mirrors, cauldrons, decorated weapons and shields. Such things have a freshness and vitality that we do not find in the contemporary products of the classical [Greek and Roman] world. Moreover, the Celts were skilled agriculturalists [farmers] and pastoralists [herders], feeding the very large population of Gaul on the produce of the land. They were especially skilled with horses, their breeding, and their use in war and for transport.[6]

A bronze statue from around 500 B.C. depicts an Etruscan warrior with metal armor and shield.

By 700 B.C., and likely even earlier, the Celts inhabiting southern Gaul had established sporadic trade with more advanced peoples living south of the Alps. For instance, Gallic traders exchanged their own luxury products for those of the Etruscans, a skilled and highly organized and urbanized people who controlled most of northern Italy at the time. Gallic contact with the classical Mediterranean world increased about the year 600, when colonists from Greece established the city of Mas-

salia, now Marseilles, on the coast of what is now southern France. The Greeks possessed many fine luxury goods, and not surprisingly, the Gauls eagerly established a vigorous trade with the newcomers.

The Greeks also had a highly advanced culture, with language, architecture, religion, and social customs that the Gauls found strange and even a bit intriguing. But while other peoples, including the Romans, absorbed many aspects of Greek culture, the Gauls resisted much of the Greek cultural influence that might have brought about significant changes in local Celtic society. This was partly because the Gauls were fiercely proud of their own Celtic heritage. Another reason that Greek influence on Gaul was minimal was that the vast majority of Gauls had only scant and indirect contact with Greek society. "Indeed," comments scholar Anthony King in his book *Roman Gaul and Germany*, large-scale Greek influence would have been unlikely "since Massalia was primarily a trading station rather than an imperialistic power. Her concern was to sell Greek artifacts and expertise, very successfully to judge from the results."[7] So the Greeks, who had no interest in conquering Gaul, confined themselves to the southern coastal region, and traditional Gallic culture remained largely unchanged.

The Gauls Menace Rome

However, while the character of Gallic culture continued intact, the society itself eventually experienced considerable upheaval. Sudden improvements in iron technology in the fifth century B.C. brought better farming methods and vastly increased food production. This, in turn, stimulated huge population increases and set in motion large-scale migrations similar to those that had swept through Europe a millennium before. As the fourth century dawned, hordes of Gauls crossed the Alps into the moist green plains of the Po Valley. Some settled there, but others pushed farther south into Etruria, the region occupied by the Etruscans, and, finally, in the year 390 to the very borders of Roman Latium.

The Romans quickly assembled a large army to stop this menace from the north. At the time the Roman army, though not nearly as formidable as it would later become, was still far more organized and better equipped and trained than the Gallic forces. As military historian J. F. C. Fuller explains:

The Gallic infantry was untrained and frequently little more than an armed rabble. The long cutting sword was their chief weapon. . . . They carried wooden or wattle [thatched] shields, and the true warrior despised armor and fought stripped. The chiefs, however, wore bronze cuirasses or coats of mail and highly decorated helmets. There was no tactical organization other than the tribal group, and few preparations were made for a campaign. There was a total lack of planning; battles were headlong assaults . . . in which the warriors rapidly ex-

Tough, bearded horsemen like these were among the nomadic Gauls that migrated across the Alps into Italy in the fourth century B.C.

hausted themselves and became disorganized; courage shattered itself on the rocks of discipline.[8]

Nevertheless, the Romans were unaware that the Gallic army lacked organization and discipline. Moreover, the Roman soldiers had never before encountered such fearsome- and determined-looking opponents. When the two armies met on July 18, 390 B.C., near the Allia River a few miles north of Rome, the naked, long-haired Gallic warriors staged a wild, screaming charge that completely terrified the Romans. The panic-stricken Roman ranks fell apart, and the Gauls proceeded to slaughter their opponents. From that time on July 18 became known to the Romans as the dark "day of Allia," an unlucky date on the calendar.

Gallic warriors terrorize Roman women who have taken refuge in a temple during the sacking of Rome by the Gauls in 390 B.C.

Afterward the Gallic army entered Rome, killed the few inhabitants who had not already fled, and burned much of the city. But the Romans were a tough, stubborn, and resourceful people who were able to withstand and bounce back from great hardships. Refusing to admit defeat, they began launching frequent small but devastating attacks on the invaders. The Gauls had sacked Rome only to steal its gold and valuables and had no intention of living in it anyway. They quickly grew tired of fighting, and after demanding and getting a large ransom of Roman gold, they withdrew to the Po Valley. This was the last time that a Gallic army directly threatened the capital.

"Our Sea"

The Gauls who had overrun Rome had been awestruck by its size and complexity. Although at the time Rome was still small, disorganized, and shabby compared to many of the more culturally advanced Greek cities around the Mediterranean, it was still by far the largest and most impressive town the Gauls had ever seen. The invaders could only guess at the functions of the many imposing stone temples and public buildings that lined the Roman streets and the Forum, or main square. A large number of these were government buildings, for the Romans had become strongly preoccupied with the concepts of law and government organization.

More than a century before, in the year 509 B.C., Rome's wealthiest and most influential landowners, the aristocratic patricians, had thrown out their king. In place of the kingship they established the

Roman Republic, in which individual Romans had a measurable say in how they were governed. Citizens, at the time only free adult males of substantial financial means, met regularly in a legislative body known as the Assembly to suggest and vote on laws. Since most of the members were patricians, the common people demanded and eventually got their own assembly, from which patricians were excluded. The voters also chose public officials, chief of whom were the two consuls. According to historian Chester G. Starr, the consuls, who served together for a term of a year,

> supervised the government at home and acted as generals abroad. Although in the field each consul usually operated independently with his own army, in Rome both had to concur [agree] if any serious political action could be taken. In critical emergencies the consuls stepped aside to make way for a single dictator with overriding powers, who was appointed for six months.[9]

Among the first few of the rarely appointed dictators was the respected patrician Marcus Camillus, who organized the resistance against the Gauls after the disaster at the Allia in 390.

With its citizen assemblies and elected officials, Rome's republican government appeared on the surface to be a democracy. But it was not. A third legislative body, the Senate, was more prestigious and powerful than the assemblies. The senators, all highborn aristocrats who served for life, formulated important state policy and advised the consuls. The senators also used their wealth and position to influence the way citizens voted in the assemblies. So the elite Senate was the real

A meeting of the early Senate, Rome's most powerful and influential government body.

power in Rome, and the republic was really an oligarchy, a government controlled by a chosen few. Nevertheless, Roman citizens—even the poorest—felt that their system, which was based on the rule of law rather than the arbitrary whims of a king, was far fairer and more admirable than systems in most other lands. As a result, most Romans were fiercely patriotic and willing to risk their lives to defend the state.

The battle at the Allia had not been the first instance of Roman soldiers' defending the state. At the time the Gauls threatened Rome, the Romans were already involved in wars with their neighbors, including the Etruscans. After recovering from the Gallic onslaught, Rome continued its aggressive policy and expanded outward from Latium. The Romans conquered several Apennine hill tribes, including the fierce Samnites in south-central Italy, and then in 285 turned on several Greek cities that had grown up in southern Italy during the preceding few centuries. By 265 Rome was master of all Italy south of the Po Valley. Next, Rome fought three bloody and costly wars against Carthage, a powerful north African trading city that controlled the western Mediterranean sea trade. Rome wrested that trade from Carthage, absorbed the Po Valley, and then launched military forays into the eastern Mediterranean, where several Greek-ruled kingdoms held sway. One by one these kingdoms fell to the increasingly powerful Roman armies. By the 140s B.C. the Romans could fully justify their arrogant new catchphrase, *mare nostrum*, "our sea," to describe the Mediterranean.

Gaul's "Three Separate Parts"

Roman expansion did not end with military and economic control of the Mediterranean, however. Many of the remote, undeveloped lands that stretched inland from the seacoasts beckoned the now highly imperialistic Roman government. In the 120s B.C. one of these regions, the fertile southernmost section of Gaul, came under Roman domination. To make their aggression appear justified, the Romans claimed they were protecting their local ally, the Greek city of Massalia, against attacks by southern Gallic tribes. In 118 the Romans founded the colony of

Narbo Martius, or Narbonne, near the coast about 120 miles west of Massalia. An area extending over two hundred miles east-west along the coast and the same distance northward through the valley of the Rhone River became a Roman province—the Narbonese. Thereafter, the area experienced a large influx of Roman farmers, traders, and businessmen. In this way extreme southern Gaul quickly became Romanized. Narbonese became known for its grapes, olives, timber, and metalware, which found their way into both Roman and non-Roman homes across the Mediterranean.

At the time of the Narbonese's creation, the remainder of Gaul was occupied by over two hundred separate tribes. Many of these shared common cultural roots and had similar customs and languages. So it became customary to lump them together into a few broad groups. This is exactly what Caesar did in writing the famous opening lines of his *Commentaries on the Gallic Wars*:

> The country of Gaul consists of three separate parts, one of which [in the far north] is inhabited by the Belgae, one [in the southwest] by the Aquitani, and one [in the central region] by the people whom we call "Gauls" but who are known in their own language as "Celts." These three peoples differ from one another in language, customs and laws. . . . The toughest soldiers come from the Belgae. This is because they are farthest away from the culture and civilized way of life of the Roman province [the Narbonese] . . . and they are also nearest to the Germans across the Rhine [the river recognized by Romans and Gauls

alike as the boundary between Gaul and the Germanic territories] and are continually waging war with them. For the same reason the Helvetii are the bravest among the Gauls [in the central region]; they too are in almost daily contact with the Germans, either fighting to keep them out of Gaul or launching attacks on them in their own territory.[10]

Though the Romans knew little about these Gallic lands and peoples beyond the Narbonese, they knew even less about another, more fabled Celtic land. This was the mysterious island of Britain, which lay off the northwest coast of the European mainland. The Britons were said to have large supplies of gold, tin, and pearls, which they traded with their fellow Celts who dwelled in what later came to be known as Brittany, the area of Gaul bordering the English Channel. By 100 B.C., the year Julius Caesar was born, only a handful of Roman traders had ventured outside the Narbonese, and none had ever visited Britain.

In the Midst of Military Strongmen

Caesar's interest in and subsequent conquest of Gaul and Britain grew out of his participation in the momentous power games that shaped the Roman political scene of his day. For centuries most Roman soldiers had been landowners whose loyalty had been to the state. But beginning in the early first century B.C., ambitious military generals increasingly gained the allegiance of Rome's armies. Powerful figures such as Gaius Marius, Caesar's uncle, and Cornelius Sulla raised large armies, made up in large degree of landless peasants, and promised them rewards of money and land upon retirement. In this way began the trend in which soldiers felt a sense of loyalty more to their own

The powerful general Cornelius Sulla leads his soldiers into Rome during the civil war of the 80s B.C. After seizing control of the city, Sulla declared himself dictator.

generals than to the state. Because ambitious generals could and did use their military power to manipulate politics and the government, this trend threatened the stability of the republic.

Young Caesar, who came from a prominent patrician family, grew up directly in the midst of this dangerous competition among military strongmen. Through marriage to Caesar's aunt, Julia, Marius became his uncle. And Caesar later married Pompeia, Sulla's granddaughter. Even while still in his teens, Caesar already had his own high ambitions, including the command of

---

Fond of Luxury, Art, and Women

In his biographical work Lives of the Twelve Caesars, *the first-century Roman historian Suetonius provided this revealing description of Julius Caesar's personal appearance, habits, likes, and dislikes.*

"He is said to have been tall of stature, with a fair complexion, shapely limbs, a somewhat full face, and keen black eyes; sound of health, except that towards the end [of his life] he was subject to sudden fainting fits and to nightmare as well. He was twice attacked by the falling sickness [epilepsy, a nervous-system disorder that causes seizures] during his campaigns. He was somewhat over-nice in the care of his person, being not only carefully trimmed and shaved, but even having unwanted facial hairs plucked out. . . . They say, too, that he was fantastic in his dress; that he wore a senator's tunic with fringed sleeves reaching to the wrist, and always had a girdle [wide belt] over it, though rather a loose one. . . . Many have written that he was very fond of elegance and luxury; that having laid the foundations of a country-house on his estate at Nemi [a lakefront village southeast of Rome] and finished it at great cost, he tore it all down because it did not suit him in every particular, . . . that he carried . . . mosaic [tiled] floors about with him on his campaigns, . . . that he was always a most enthusiastic collector of gems, carvings, statues, and pictures by early artists. . . . He was so . . . strict in the management of his household . . . that he put his baker in irons for serving him with one kind of bread and his guests with another. . . . That he was unbridled [unrestrained] and extravagant in his intrigues [sexual affairs] is the general opinion, and that he seduced many illustrious women."

---

armies and election to the consulship. Wisely, he took his time and worked his way up through the ranks, serving in a number of increasingly important public offices and carefully crafting a popular public image. "In Rome," wrote first-century historian Plutarch in his *Life of Caesar,*

> Caesar won a brilliant reputation and great popularity. . . . He had an ability to make himself liked which was remarkable in one of his age, and he was very much in the good graces of the ordinary citizen because of his easy manners and the friendly way in which he mixed with people. Then there were his dinner parties and entertainments and a certain splendor about his whole way of life; all this made him gradually more and more important politically.[11]

In 62 B.C. Caesar served as praetor, or overseer of the laws, courts, and justice, a post second in prestige only to that of consul. But he found his way to the top blocked by the two most powerful men in Rome—the renowned military general Gnaeus Pompey and the wealthy financier Marcus Crassus. Not discouraged, Caesar surprised the Roman world by forming an alliance with his two rivals. Singly each of these men lacked the money and influence to overshadow the power of the Senate, which distrusted all three. But by combining their resources into a partnership, which later became known as the First Triumvirate, they were able to manipulate the government to their own ends. In 60 B.C., backed by Pompey's and Crassus's supporters as well as his own, Caesar won the

A meeting of the members of the powerful political partnership, the First Triumvirate—Gnaeus Pompey, Julius Caesar, and Marcus Crassus.

consulship for the following year. He and his fellow triumvirs then ran roughshod over the Senate and other republican institutions, often ignoring and violating legislative laws and employing a small army of thugs to silence the opposition.

A Fortunate Stroke of Luck

But unlike many other ambitious men who succeed in attaining great power, Caesar was neither self-satisfied nor overconfident. He wisely looked to the future and realized that he lacked the military backing he would need to retain his grip on the government for any length of time. Clearly, to help enforce his will and fulfill his ambitions after his consulship was over, he would need his own loyal army. Perhaps more than any Roman political leader before him, Caesar had a brilliant grasp of military matters and understood the tremendous potential of the Roman army as a tool for gaining power.

As Caesar knew well, the army had undergone considerable changes in recent centuries. During early republican times soldiers were mainly landowners of Italian birth. They entered the service when the government called on them during an emergency and then returned to their farms when the fighting ended. Later, as military campaigns grew longer and took the troops farther from home, the government began paying the soldiers, many of whom became career professionals. The early army consisted of large units called legions, each having about 4,200 men. A typical legion had smaller subdivisions of 100 men each, called centuries. Each century was headed by an officer with the title of centurion and his second in command, the *optio*. When arrayed on the battlefield, the legions broke down into fighting units called maniples, most of which contained about 120 soldiers.

The considerably more efficient later republican army resulted largely from the military reforms instituted in the early first century by Gaius Marius. Under Marius soldiers did not have to own property, thus opening up military service to many lower-class Romans who otherwise would have been unemployed. Marius also increased the soldiers' pay, made training more rigorous, and standardized both training and weapons. Generals after Marius, including Caesar, began recruiting large numbers of non-Italians from the empire's provinces, so such standardization helped to unify troops of diverse cultural backgrounds. Most legions in the later republican army had five to six thousand men, broken down into centuries of eighty, rather than one hundred, men each. The principal battlefield unit was the cohort, which had replaced the maniple. A typical legion had ten cohorts—a specialized one made up of ten centuries, and nine others having six or seven centuries each. Each century broke down into ten *contubernia*. Consisting of eight men who shared the same tent and traveled and ate together, the *contubernium* was the equivalent of the modern army platoon.

Caesar realized that the best way to acquire the command of his own army was to become proconsul, or governor, of one of the Roman provinces, each of which had a small contingent of troops. By raising new recruits and leading some kind of successful military campaign, he could gain both glory and the allegiance of his troops. Attaining a proconsulship would also make it impossible for the Senate to arrest him later for breaking laws while he was consul. This was because Roman law prohibited the state from prosecuting governors, consuls, and other high officials for past offenses while they served in office.

With all of this in mind, while still consul in 59 B.C. Caesar used his power and influence to get not one, but two

Roman legionnaires. The one at left holds a cornu, *a curved battle trumpet, while the other wears a* lorca segmentata, *a leather tunic with attached metal strips.*

provinces. One was Cisalpine Gaul, the long since Romanized Po Valley. The other was Illyricum, the sparsely inhabited territory directly across the narrow Adriatic Sea from the eastern Italian coast. Caesar had no sooner gained control over these provinces, and for a period of five years instead of the customary one, when he had a fortunate stroke of luck. The governor of the Narbonese, beyond the Alps, died suddenly. Wasting no time, Caesar intimidated the government into granting him the Narbonese, too.

Also fortunate for Caesar was the fact that at the very time that he acquired control of the Narbonese, unrest among some of the tribes north of that province

Avoiding Utter Ruin

Part of Caesar's strategy in obtaining governorships of provinces was to ensure that he could continually remain in high office and thereby escape criminal prosecution. In this excerpt from his biography of Caesar, historian Michael Grant explains:

"The various acts of violence and other improprieties which he had committed during his tenure [term of service] of the consulship meant that, from now onwards, he could only, according to Roman law, avoid utter ruin by remaining continually in public office: for if ever, even for a moment, he lost the immunity conferred by such an office, then prosecution for a variety of offences, including high treason, would immediately descend on him and his ruin would be assured. This future prospect became abundantly clear during the very first days after the conclusion of his consular year, when two of the new praetors proposed to the Senate that all his acts . . . as consul should be declared invalid and formally cancelled. In three speeches . . . Caesar dealt with his enemies' charges and endeavored to rebut them. Then, however, without waiting for the Senate's decision, he considered it advisable to move outside Rome, since once away from the capital he was already a governor exempted from prosecution. And so . . . he spent three months completing the preparations for his impending campaigns in Transalpine Gaul."

appeared to threaten Roman interests. That, he reasoned, would give him an excuse for the military campaign he desired. According to Suetonius, Caesar was so happy over getting the Narbonese that "he could not keep from boasting a few days later before a crowded house that

[he had] gained his heart's desire to the grief . . . of his opponents [in the Senate]."[12] In the last days of 59 B.C., with his consulship drawing to a close, Caesar began drawing up his plans for the conquests that would, in the fullness of time, bring him eternal fame.

Chapter

2 Caesar the Imperialist: The Beginning of Old Gaul's End

When the forty-two-year-old Julius Caesar arrived in Cisalpine Gaul to assume his proconsulship early in 58 B.C., he eagerly anticipated the years ahead. His immediate goals were to establish himself as a great and famous general and to build a large, strong, and loyal personal army. These accomplishments, he hoped, would ensure his long-range goal—namely, to retain and increase the size of his powerful voice in Roman government affairs.

The military task Caesar faced in Gaul was huge and daunting. Most of Transalpine Gaul, which stretched for hundreds of miles north and west of the Roman Narbonese, was rugged, heavily forested, and unknown territory. The area swarmed with diverse tribes having strange languages, customs, and attitudes, peoples the Romans saw as barbarians and who, in turn, looked on the Romans with suspicion, hostility, or both.

Considering the unknowns and dangers he faced, Caesar had no way of predicting how long his Gallic campaigns would take. It is not even certain whether he originally intended to conquer all of Transalpine Gaul or just enough of it to accomplish his immediate goals. He could not have guessed at the time that almost eight long years of exhausting and dangerous campaigns lay ahead. The first phase

of these campaigns, lasting from early 58 to late 56, would lead him and his men into bloody battles as far north as what is now Belgium and as far west as the Atlantic coast. This opening salvo of Caesar's Gallic conquests would spell the beginning of the end of the Celtic way of life in the "old Gaul" and foreshadow the Romanized western Europe to come.

Formulating an Effective Strategy

It is likely that Caesar thought little of the cultural upheavals his military exploits would produce in Gaul. A prime example of a Roman imperialist, he firmly believed that it was Rome's destiny to dominate what were considered "inferior" non-Roman peoples. In his view the Gauls would one day thank the Romans for "civilizing" them; therefore, he saw his plans for their conquest as a humane crusade rather than the unprovoked aggression it really was.

Always swift and decisive once his mind was made up, Caesar wasted no time in implementing these plans. In the first few months of 58, he took command of Cisalpine Gaul's military forces, which consisted of three legions, or groups of five to six thousand soldiers. Leaving recruiters behind to raise more troops from this province, he marched his legions westward into his other Gallic province, the Narbonese. There he collected another legion, giving him a total initial force of no more than twenty-four thousand troops. This, he knew, was much too small a number to conquer, organize, and police a territory as large as Transalpine Gaul. To build up his forces to the levels he needed, Caesar planned to maintain a steady stream of new recruits from his three provinces.

Caesar was well aware, however, that to achieve success both in Gaul and back home in Rome he needed more than just large numbers of troops. He needed a well-thought-out and effective strategy that would both capitalize on his own strengths and play on his enemies' weaknesses. Regarding his strategy for Gaul, for instance,

A Roman cameo depicting Julius Caesar wearing a laurel wreath, in many ancient lands a symbol of victory, honor, and glory.

he correctly reasoned that the key to winning a long, drawn-out campaign in a remote land was maintaining adequate supply trains. Most armies up to that time, including many Roman ones, attempted to win quick, decisive victories. They hoped to live off what they could carry or what they could forage in the areas where they fought. So they often failed to create the organization of supply bases and transports necessary to move the massive amounts of food needed for an army on a long campaign. By recognizing the supply problem from the start, Caesar demonstrated his remarkable, innate grasp of military affairs. As James Breasted puts it:

> He knew that the greatest problem facing a commander was to keep his army in supplies and to guard against moving it to a point where it was impossible either to carry with it the supplies for feeding it or to find them on the spot. So efficient was his own great organization that he knew he could transport supplies more successfully than could the . . . Gauls. He perceived that no great [Gallic] host could be kept long together in one place, because they did not possess the organization for carrying with them, or securing later, enough food to maintain them long. When the necessity of finding provisions . . . forced them to separate into smaller armies, then Caesar [would] swiftly advance and defeat these smaller divisions.[13]

In addition to this divide-and-conquer approach in Gaul, Caesar also worked out a strategy to maintain his power base in Rome. The very real chance existed that his political enemies, perhaps including his ambitious partners in the triumvirate,

A bust of Gnaeus Pompey, who gained fame and glory fighting pirates and rebellious slaves in the 70s and 60s B.C. He remained a powerful figure in Rome while Caesar was away in Gaul.

known, throughout most of ancient times the Celtic peoples of Europe did not maintain written records or histories. Thus, Caesar's *Commentaries*, supplemented by a few other brief Greek and Roman sources, constitutes the major surviving written description of the first-century B.C. Gallic and German societies he was about to annihilate.

Despite his personal disdain for the Gauls and Germans he encountered, Caesar took a keen interest in their military and social customs as well as their peculiar tribal organization. Concerning the latter his *Commentaries* reveals that most of the Gallic tribes were governed by oligarchies, or ruling groups of nobles. A few tribes, for instance the Remi, one of the leading branches of the Belgae of northern Gaul, had kings. But by Caesar's time such a monarch was little more than the most influential local oligarch, whose decisions were usually questioned and guided by the other nobles. Each noble looked after his own local interests, including the peasants who lived and worked on the lands he controlled. This widespread allegiance to local rather than central authority contributed to the overall lack of political organization that made the Gauls vulnerable to conquest by the Romans. The only unifying element among the various tribes was the small priest class, the Druids. These highly respected and even feared figures apparently conducted the religious rituals and also acted as judges, settling disputes between neighboring tribes.

By contrast, the Germanic tribes were ruled by chiefs who permitted no one to own land on a permanent basis. The exact reasons for this restriction remain unclear, but it seems that the Germans looked with scorn on settled agricultural life, believing

Crassus and Pompey, might try to undermine his position while he was away. So he could not afford to be out of touch with Rome and its political intrigues for too long. Caesar dealt with this problem in two ways, the first of which was his regularly updated journal—the *Commentaries*. To make sure that both senators and ordinary citizens had constant reminders of his triumphs, he sent periodic installments of the journal back to Rome.

A Keen Interest in the Enemy

As it turned out, Caesar's journal proved to be valuable in a way that he himself never dreamed of. As far as is currently that full-time farmers like the Gauls had lost "essential" elements of manhood, including warlike zeal. For this reason many German family heads remained hunters rather than farmers. Since growing some food was still a necessity, the chiefs assigned plots of land to certain individuals for intervals of a year, at the end of which the farmers surrendered the plots back to the community. Like the Gauls, the Germanic tribes of Caesar's time recognized no overall central authority, so they lacked the unity that might have made them a serious military threat to Roman borders.

Besides his planned use of the *Commentaries* as propaganda, Caesar devised

Gallic horsemen like this one were effective fighters, a fact that motivated Caesar to enlist conquered Gauls in his Roman cavalry.

another way to help maintain his power base in Rome. He set up a network of agents and messengers headed by his trusted and able assistants, Cornelius Balbus and Gaius Oppius. According to scholar Lily Ross Taylor in her book *Party Politics in the Age of Caesar*, in Caesar's day Rome had

> no police force, no postal or freight service, and, except in the treasury, practically no civil service. The nobles looked after their personal safety by keeping up bands of followers and attendants. They communicated with the cities of Italy and the provinces through personal messengers, using vehicles [chariots or wagons], horses, or ships which were their private property. . . . Caesar's organization of his contacts in Rome through the loyal Balbus was remarkably efficient during his years of absence in Gaul. There was a steady stream of messengers between Rome and Gaul, and Caesar was informed of everything [that happened in Italy]. Balbus, later aided by the equally efficient Oppius, did wonders in upholding Caesar's influence and seeing to it that the men [in Rome] whom Caesar supported lived up to their obligations.[14]

"No Friends of Ours"

Once his vital link to the capital was securely in place, Caesar turned his attention to a potentially dangerous situation that was developing just north of the Narbonese. At the time, the Helvetii, a Gallic people occupying what is now northern and western Switzerland, were in the midst

Nothing Less than a Masterpiece

Caesar's military journal, the Commentaries, *has been translated, read, and studied extensively by both scholars and students through the ages. The following description and insightful critique of the work is by the prolific historian Michael Grant in his excellent biography, titled simply* Caesar.

"The *Gallic War* and subsequent *Civil War* were [together] entitled *Commentaries*, a term which, with unwarranted modesty, deliberately falls somewhat short of 'Histories,' denoting rather a set of commander's dispatches or memoranda, amplified partly by speeches (intended as always in antiquity [ancient times] to give background rather than represent exact words). . . . Caesar's enormous brain power and exceedingly lucid [clear], compact, Latin style transform this apparently unambitious work into nothing less than a major masterpiece. The fact that the Roman commander-in-chief was its author (except for the last of its eight books, which was written by one of his generals, Aulus Hirtius) brings great advantages and disadvantages alike. The advantages lie in the extraordinary authority conferred by the author's unique inside knowledge, and by all the manifold [diverse] talents which he could bring to bear upon its presentation to the reader. The disadvantages reside in Caesar's personal preoccupations [interests and biases], and most of all his desire to refute his political enemies in Rome. This sometimes induced him to magnify, minimize, and distort—though it is usually the implications [the way he interprets or judges the importance of the facts] rather than the facts [themselves] that suffer, since Caesar . . . was far too good a hand at publicity to lie more than was absolutely necessary."

of a great social upheaval. Under increasing pressure from warlike German tribes from the eastern side of the Rhine the Helvetii felt they had no choice but to pack up and move westward. As Caesar recorded in his journal, the tribe, more than 300,000 strong, was preparing "all the necessary arrangements for a mass migration. They were to buy up all the wagons and pack animals that they could, sow as much grain as possible so as to have adequate supplies on the march, and make treaties of friendship with neighboring states."[15]

Caesar and other Roman leaders were convinced that the Helvetii's impending migration would pass through and ravage the northern portion of the Narbonese. Whether or not the Helvetii actually intended to cross through the Roman province and, if so, whether they posed a

This drawing depicts the Helvetii leaders planning their mass migration through Gaul. They told Caesar that their intentions were peaceable and that they wanted only to pass through Roman lands briefly on their way west.

threat to the region, remains unclear. Caesar claimed:

> When they heard of my arrival [in the Narbonese], the Helvetii sent a deputation [delegation] of their chief men to see me. . . . [They said] that their intentions in marching through the Province were entirely peaceable; there simply existed no alternative route; and they asked me to allow them to do so without raising any objections. . . . It did not seem to me that any concessions ought to be made to such people; they were no friends of ours, and I did not believe that, if they got the chance of marching through the Province, they would refrain from acts of robbery and violence.[16]

Despite this claim, the Helvetii *did* have an alternative route westward. This was to the north of the Narbonese, through the region inhabited by the Aedui tribe, which was on friendly terms with the Romans. Caesar went on to say that the Aedui, fearing they would be overrun by the Helvetii, begged him to stop this advancing "menace." Though it is now impossible to be certain of the real facts, it is highly doubtful that the Helvetii, no matter which route they were considering, intended to do anyone any harm. That they were themselves the victims of harassment by the Germans *is* certain. And there seems no reason to question their claim that they merely wanted to find new homes in the western lands near the Atlantic coast. Moreover, a secret agreement between Caesar and the Aedui, though undocumented, seems probable. Such an agreement would block both routes west, forcing the Helvetii to violate either Roman or Aedui territory and giving Caesar an excuse to attack the migrating tribe.

Caesar's First Battle

Whatever the course of the preliminary events, in April 58 B.C. Caesar did attack the Helvetii. About three-quarters of the tribe had already crossed the Saône River, on the eastern border of Aedui territory, when, as Caesar told it,

> I set out from camp soon after midnight with four legions and approached that division of the enemy which had not yet crossed the river. They were hampered by their baggage and our attack took them by surprise. We killed great numbers of them.[17]

Because only a small fraction of this Helvetian contingent consisted of warriors, who in any case had no time to organize a credible resistance, the attack was less a battle and more a massacre of helpless people.

A few weeks later Caesar caught up with the rest of the Helvetii, and this time a mass of warriors, perhaps as many as forty to fifty thousand gathered to resist the Romans. Caesar now faced the first important challenge of his military career. According to J. F. C. Fuller, it was

> to be Caesar's first battle, and his whole future depended, not on winning it but on *not* losing it. So far, he had had little experience of war; his reputation was still to be made; he was new to his men; his . . . four veteran legions, some 20,000 to 24,000 men in all, were faced with an enemy numerically vastly

An Underestimated Culture

Like other Romans, Caesar tended to look upon many foreign peoples as inferior and even uncivilized. This was certainly his opinion of the rustic Gauls. However, as historian Donald R. Dudley explains in his book The Romans, 850 B.C.–A.D. 337, *the Gauls were far from being uncivilized.*

"The free society of Celtic Gaul which Caesar was about to demolish was the most advanced culture which had yet appeared north of the Alps. It was commonly underestimated by classical [Greek and Roman] writers, since it lacked some of the features which they regarded as essential for civilization. It had no cities, for example . . . although centers of population had begun to grow up round the dwellings of powerful nobles, or for purposes of trade and industry. . . . Socially, the Celtic world was dominated by great nobles living on their country estates with their kinsmen and vassals [dependent workers]. They had long valued the luxury products of the classical world, especially its wine and metalware. But the Celts were themselves skilled workers in metals—iron, bronze, and gold. . . . Moreover, the Celts were skilled agriculturalists, . . . feeding the very large population of Gaul on the produce of the land. They were especially skilled with horses, their breeding, and their use in war and for transport."

This depiction of the Helvetii's migration, produced many centuries after the real event, inaccurately shows the tribesmen clad in European garb of a later period.

superior to them. But one thing stood in his favor; accompanied as the Helvetian warriors were by vast numbers of women, children, cattle, and wagons, their mobility was severely restricted. Were he to do no more than repulse [their charge], they could not escape him; sooner or later their supplies would fail them, and then they would be at his mercy.[18]

Sure enough, the Helvetian warriors' dependence on and need to protect their wagon train proved to be their downfall. As the battle opened, these warriors launched an enthusiastic charge. But the Romans countered with a barrage of spears, which pierced the flimsy Gallic shields, forcing many of their owners to cast them aside and fight only with swords. The gallant but poorly equipped and disorganized warriors quickly grew exhausted and retreated. They soon regrouped and attacked again, but once more the Romans' superior organization, armor, and weapons overcame them. The Helvetii then fell back to their wagon train, which

Caesar's men ferociously assaulted for the rest of the day and into the night. As in the previous engagement at the Saône, wholesale slaughter ensued.

Caesar's victory in his first Gallic campaign abruptly halted the Helvetian migration, and the survivors returned to their homes in the Alpine foothills. In all, Caesar claimed in his *Commentaries*, his men had slain 258,000 members of the tribe. There is little doubt that this incredibly huge figure was an exaggeration designed to impress his readers back in Italy. The actual number of Helvetian casualties was more likely in the range of 60,000 to 80,000, which was nevertheless one of the largest and most tragic death tolls in Rome's long record of blatant imperialism. Roman generals, though often brutal, did not routinely slaughter their enemies in such great numbers. Caesar's reasons for doing so will never be known for certain, but it is probable that he wanted this, his first real military campaign, to make him a man to be feared by all. In this endeavor he succeeded.

3 Gaul's Savage Frontiers: The Peace of the Sword Descends

Caesar's merciless defeat of the Helvetii was only the first step in his planned conquest of Gaul. In the summer of 58 B.C., the Romans occupied only a small portion of the Gallic lands beyond the Narbonese. To the north and west stretched thousands of square miles of rolling forested hills and fertile valleys, in his view all ripe for Roman picking. And to the east and northeast, the mighty Rhine River meandered for hundreds of miles, marking the traditional border between the Gallic and German lands. All along this savage frontier dwelled Gallic and Germanic tribes that had not yet tasted Roman steel. Caesar decided that their lands, forts, houses, crops, animals, and indeed they themselves should belong to Rome.

In his own mind Caesar needed no excuse for such naked aggression. He lived in an age when the idea of the strong oppressing and controlling the weak was accepted as the natural order of things. Yet, as he had learned to do in Rome's corridors of political power, he carefully and methodically justified each campaign, attack, and conquest as being "necessary." His conquests were never motivated by personal reasons, he publicly maintained. Instead, they were unavoidable actions forced upon him by circumstances beyond his control. His justification for moving

A bust of Julius Caesar, who justified his conquest of the Helvetii and other Gallic peoples as necessary for the good of both Rome and Gaul.

against the Helvetii, for instance, had been that they had posed a threat to both Romans and Gauls. "I had been avenging wrongs done in the past by the Helvetii to Rome," he stated in his journal.

Nevertheless, Gaul had benefited just as much as Rome by the result, since the Helvetii, when things were going perfectly well with them, had left their own country with the express purpose of making war on the whole of Gaul and bringing it into subjection to them.[19]

This explanation, of course, was untrue. But Caesar's Roman readers accepted it, as did even some of the Gallic chiefs who had feared that the Helvetii migration might threaten their own lands. Caesar planned to use similar justifications as he continued his thrust into the wilds of Gaul.

"Caesar Ought to Come to Me"

Before launching any further attacks, however, Caesar saw the wisdom of accepting willing Gauls as Roman allies. The natives knew the country better than he did, after all, and this could prove an invaluable aid in his campaigns. He did not have to wait long for the first such allies to come forward. With the Helvetii out of the way, the Aedui had emerged as the dominant tribe in central Gaul, and the Aedui chiefs now promised to support Caesar in his endeavors.

At the same time, the Aedui chiefs, along with leaders of other tribes in the region, requested that Caesar stop the Germanic tribes, especially the fierce and much feared Suebi, whose raids into eastern Gaul were steadily growing in number and severity. In his journal Caesar quoted the Aeduan spokesman as saying that the German leader, Ariovistus,

had behaved like an arrogant and cruel tyrant. He demanded as hostages the children of all the Gallic nobles, and would inflict every sort of torture on them if everything were not done precisely according to his will and pleasure. The man was a savage, incapable of controlling his passions and ambitions; it was impossible to put up with his tyranny any longer.[20]

Caesar agreed to deal with the Suebi, but not because he cared about Ariovistus's reported atrocities, or acts of extreme cruelty. Once more wisely looking toward the future, Caesar recognized that the Germans would continue to be a threat to the Romanized Gaul he was trying to create. As Plutarch described it, "The Germans were quite intolerable neighbors to the tribes under Caesar's control. It appeared certain that, once they got the chance, they would . . . spread over the frontiers [borders] and occupy Gaul."[21]

As usual, Caesar wasted little time. In the autumn of 58 B.C. he advanced with six legions toward the western side of the Rhine, where Ariovistus was camped with an army and a huge host of Suebi women and children. The Roman leader decided it would be wise to take his opponent's measure before engaging him in battle. So he invited Ariovistus to a face-to-face meeting. According to Caesar's journal, after receiving the invitation, the German replied:

If I wanted anything from Caesar I would go to him; if Caesar wants anything from me, then he ought to come to me. . . . In any case I cannot understand what sort of business Caesar, or the Roman people for that matter, can have with my part of Gaul—mine by right of conquest.[22]

To this, Caesar replied:

> I must . . . make the following requests: First, that you bring no more forces of Germans across the Rhine. Secondly, that you give back the Aeduan hostages [taken to ensure that the Aedui would not attack the Germans] which you now hold. . . . Thirdly, that you . . . do no harm to the Aedui and . . . enter into no hostilities either with them or their allies. If you accept these terms, you can be sure that you will never lose the friendship and good will both of myself and of the Roman people. If you reject them, then I shall have to act.[23]

Ariovistus, in turn, offered this reply—an arrogant and overconfident threat that sealed his fate:

> In war it is a recognized thing that the conqueror can dictate his own terms to the conquered. Certainly Rome has always governed her own subjects in her own way without waiting to be told what to do by someone else. And, just as I am giving Rome no instructions about how to exercise her proper rights, so Rome should refrain from interfering with me in the exercise of mine. As for the Aedui, they took the risk of going to war with me and were defeated in battle. They now [must]

A later European engraving depicts the encampments of Caesar (left) and Ariovistus in the autumn of 58 B.C.

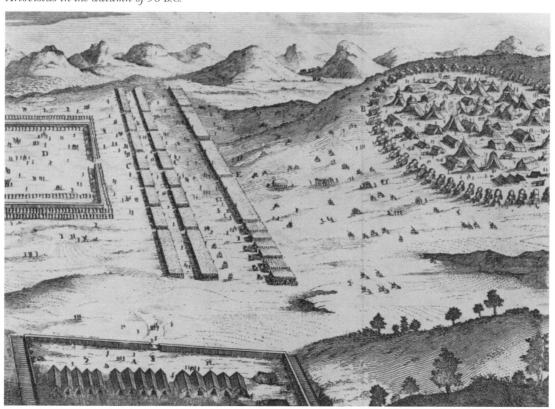

Ariovistus (left, on horseback) unwisely boasts of his power and valor to Caesar (the other horseman) shortly before the battle in which the Romans annihilated most of the Germanic war leader's tribe.

pay tribute to me. . . . You threaten me. . . . Let me tell you that so far no one has made war on me without being destroyed. You may attack whenever you like. You will then discover what can be done by the valor of German soldiers who have never been conquered in war, who are perfectly trained in arms, and who for fourteen years have never sheltered beneath a roof.[24]

Ariovistus's arrogant threats failed to frighten Caesar, who now ordered his legionnaires into action. As the Roman army advanced on the enemy's position, however, the German leader suddenly seemed to soften his warlike stance and himself called for talks. These meetings broke down when Caesar discovered that the German cavalry was harassing and threatening his men even as the conference was in progress. Feeling that his opponent had tested his patience too much, the Roman leader wasted no more energy on diplomacy. After a few days of strategic maneuvering, the Romans attacked and engaged the German warriors in a savage battle. "When the signal was given," wrote Caesar,

> our men rushed forward so fiercely and the enemy came on so swiftly and furiously that there was no time for hurling our spears. They were thrown aside, and the fighting was with swords at close quarters. The Germans adopted their usual close formation to defend themselves from the sword thrusts, but many of our men were brave enough to leap right on top of the wall of shields, tear the shields from the hands that held them, and stab down at the enemy from above.[25]

Like their distant relatives the Gauls, the Germans were tough and fearless fighters but lacked discipline and training. After an hour or two the German ranks crumbled, and Caesar and his men pursued the retreating enemy for over forty miles, slaughtering stragglers all along the way.

Unfortunately for the Germans their main camp was located in the path of the

The Tools of a Soldier's Trade

The extreme efficiency and devastating power of Caesar's legions were due partly to the soldiers' expert use of lethal, and at the same time flexible, weapons and armor. In his detailed biography of Caesar, historian Ernle Bradford offers this overview of what he calls a first-century B.C. Roman legionnaire's "tools of the trade."

By the time of Caesar the arms of the legionnaire had been streamlined . . . into two only—the sword and spear. Swords were basically of a type that the Romans had first encountered in Spain. They had a double cutting edge and a stabbing-point, were sheathed in a metal-bound leather scabbard, and hung on the legionnaire's right hand side . . . . The spears came in two main types; both were throwing spears known as a *pilum,* and one was light-weight and the other a heavy-weight. . . . The Caesarian legionnaire was protected by a mail shirt [made of thin, jointed metal links or plates] that hung about half way down his thighs, under which he wore a leather jerkin [sleeveless jacket], and on his head what is called a Montefortino helmet (so-called after the cemetery where an example was found). This type of helmet had protective cheek pieces and was pear-shaped, rising to a lead-filled topknot which held a horsehair crest. A rim ran around the bottom of the helmet, swept out farther at the back to protect the neck against glancing blows. The shield was oval-shaped and . . . was made from laminated [coated] strips of wood. . . . Shields were often leather covered. . . . Greaves [lower-leg armor] were rarely worn by the ordinary legionnaire, and his equipment ended in his heavy leather sandals . . . laced over the foot and up around the ankles, the soles studded with iron nails."

A Roman officer wears a vest of chain mail with leather shoulder pieces, a woolen cape, a metal helmet with protective cheek guards, and a standard two-foot-long sword.

Roman onslaught. In an orgy of murder and destruction, Caesar's legionnaires annihilated the camp, killing most of the women and children. Among the dead were Ariovistus's two wives and his daughter. The German leader, perhaps badly wounded, made it across the Rhine but died soon afterward. The Roman victory and subsequent massacre, an atrocity far worse than any attributed to Ariovistus, sent a wave of fear through the region. "The great reputation of the Suebi was destroyed," writes Ernle Bradford. "Only the scattering of a few German tribes, of little importance in themselves, was left in Gaul. For many years to come it was as if a great silence hung over the grand, divisive river of the Rhine. The peace of the sword had descended."[26]

A Fierce and Courageous People

In fact, that peace now spread over all of central and southern Gaul, for the Gallic tribes clearly had the same awe and fear of Caesar's wrath that the Germans did. Caesar rightly sensed that the first phase of his Gallic campaigns was at an end. After wintering in Cisalpine Gaul, he turned his attention to the reputedly fierce Belgae tribes in the northern reaches of Transalpine Gaul. In the summer of 57 B.C., he led eight legions, perhaps 45,000 to 50,000 men, to the Aisne River in what is now northeastern France. The various branches of the Belgae had, of course, heard about Caesar's recent aggressions against their southern neighbors. For a while Belgian leaders talked boldly of uniting in an all-out effort to repulse the Ro-

mans. Had this happened, the tribes could have fielded as many as 300,000 warriors, a force that even Caesar might not have been able to defeat.

However, just as Caesar had anticipated, the lack of organized supply trains in Gaul worked to his advantage. Each Belgian tribe was used to living off of its own local and barely adequate seasonal harvest. No intertribe organization, food stockpiles, or even regional supply bases existed in the region, and feeding a huge united army for more than a few days was simply impossible. Realizing this, many of the tribes submitted to Caesar without a fight. Among these were the Remi, Bellovaci, Suessiones, and Ambiani. A few Belgian tribes decided to fight, but here Caesar had the advantage of being able to pick off relatively small, weak forces one at a time and gain easy victories.

However, Caesar found one group of Belgae far from easy to subdue. These were the Nervii, who staged a resistance so savage and courageous that Roman historians recalled it vividly for generations to come. In his *Commentaries* Caesar gave this description of one of the toughest enemies he would ever face:

> Beyond the frontiers of the Ambiani live the Nervii. I inquired what sort of people they were and how they lived, and received the following information. No traders ever came into their country because they did not allow wine to be imported or any other luxury, in the belief that indulgences of this sort make men feeble-spirited and lacking in courage. A fierce people and extremely courageous, they were very bitter in their denunciations [verbal attacks] of the other Belgae for having

This portion of a Roman frieze, or decorative sculptured panel, shows a struggle between Romans and Gauls.

forgotten the traditional courage of their race and given in to Rome. As to themselves, they had declared that they would never send envoys to us and never accept any kind of peace.[27]

The proud Nervii gathered their full force of at least sixty thousand warriors and laid an ambush for the Romans. As Caesar approached the Sambre River on the southern edge of Nervii territory, he ordered his main force to make camp and sent a scouting party of cavalry across the river. The Romans were not anticipating an attack and could not see the thousands of nearly naked warriors hiding on a thickly wooded hillside. Suddenly these fighters burst forth, and as Caesar described it, they

rushed out of the woods in full force and charged down on our cavalry, whom they brushed aside and routed

[defeated] with the utmost ease. They then swept on down to the river, moving at such an incredible speed that to us it looked as though they were at the edge of the woods, in the river, and on top of us all in the same moment. With the same extraordinary speed they swarmed up the opposite hill toward our camp and fell upon the men who were engaged in fortifying it.[28]

The onset of battle was so sudden that many of Caesar's men had no time even to put on their helmets and armor, and most found themselves in small groups, separated from their centurions and other unit leaders. In the desperate, hand-to-hand death struggle that followed, Caesar himself lunged into the fray. He ran from one Roman contingent to another, organizing and encouraging his men. As in earlier Roman-Gallic encounters, superior

Caesar's Officers

Caesar's military successes in Gaul and in later campaigns were due in part to his efficient organization of his cohorts, or army units, and to the various kinds of officers who commanded these units. In his essay "The Roman Army of the Later Republic," in Warfare in the Ancient World, *historian Lawrence Keppie comments:*

"In battle the standard formation for the legion or group of legions was the traditional three lines. On one occasion only, in his later commentaries on the Civil War, does Caesar provide details of the disposition [arrangement] of cohorts. . . . He placed four cohorts in the front line, and three in each of the other two; but other dispositions could be adopted if the circumstances demanded. The cohorts of the third line were kept as a reserve, in the role of the old *triarii* [experienced veterans]. The backbone of the army were the centurions [unit leaders], promoted from the ranks, whom Caesar saw as the conduit [transmitter] of his views [and orders] to the rank and file. The legion's chief centurion was drawn from their number, and held this post for one year only, thereafter reverting to his former rank. The tribunes [popularly elected officials], more aristocratic in origin and outlook, were less reliable; they held no executive commands [high military ranks]. Caesar's use of his legates [provincial officials] adds much to our understanding of their role. They were young senators, some without prior military experience; those who stayed loyal to Caesar enjoyed his patronage in the years that followed. The legates were employed in a variety of tasks, commanding small expeditions or building parties, geographical areas or individual legions, or groups of legions. The post of 'legionary legate' grew out of this system."

training and weaponry eventually turned the tide of battle in the Romans' favor. But the defiant and heroic Nervii stood their ground and refused to retreat. In a horrendous bloodbath they died by the thousands. According to Caesar's journal:

The enemy's position was now entirely hopeless, yet they showed quite extraordinary courage. When their front ranks had fallen, those behind stepped forward onto the bodies of the dead and fought from on top of them. When these men also were cut down and the corpses piled up in heaps, the survivors still stood as if upon a mound, hurling their weapons down at us or catching our spears and throwing them back again. Indeed, one must say that these were people of absolutely outstanding courage. Their daring had carried them across a very broad river, up the steep banks on the other side, and then forward against a strong defensive position. Certainly their spirit must have been great to make light of such difficulties as these. So ended this battle, by which the name and nation of the Nervii were virtually wiped out.[29]

With the Belgae, supposedly the fiercest of the Gauls, seemingly pacified, Caesar had reason to hope that his conquest of Gaul was largely finished. He set up local administrative systems, placing the Aedui chief in charge of central Gaul and the Remi chief in charge of the Belgian lands. These leaders were ordered to keep the peace in their respective areas and meet with Caesar for further orders on a regular basis. Satisfied with this arrangement, Caesar spent the winter of 57–56 B.C., as he had the previous one, in Cisalpine Gaul. He could not return to Rome, since if he left his provinces, his authority as proconsul would become null and void and the Senate would surely arrest him for past offenses.

Cracks in the Triumvirate

It was from a safe distance, then, that Caesar attended to the political situation in Rome that winter. He had been the one who had shrewdly persuaded Crassus and Pompey to form the triumvirate in the first place and was, therefore, in a sense the glue that held the grand alliance together. With Caesar gone from the capital so long, the triumvirs had become increasingly suspicious of one another, and their partnership had begun to deteriorate. Making matters worse, some leading senators, sensing cracks forming in the triumvirate, had recently been trying to play one triumvir against another.

It finally became clear to Caesar and his partners that they needed a face-to-face meeting to patch up their differences. In April 56 B.C. Crassus and Pompey traveled to Luca, in the southern part of Cisalpine Gaul, and there the three men promised to sustain the unity of the triumvirate. They agreed that each should receive some token of power to appease his personal ambitions. In Caesar's case, this consisted of an extension of his proconsulships for another five years in order to ensure him plenty of time for further campaigns.

Although Caesar's brief stay at Luca is famous for the meeting of the triumvirs, a number of other noteworthy meetings took place at the same time. Caesar's Gallic conquests had cemented his powerful position in Roman politics, and many important Romans journeyed to Luca to pay him homage or to seek favors from him. Among these were the governors of the provinces of Sardinia and Spain, nearly 200 senators, and 120 lictors, prestigious civil officials. Some senators—those who wanted to see the triumvirs' powers limited—either did not attend the gathering or held their tongues for fear of angering Caesar. Other public officials outdid themselves praising him and granting him honors and money. As Plutarch pointed out in this excerpt from his *Life of Caesar*, most of the senators who voted Caesar public money did so because the presence of the triumvirs, as well as of Pompey's and Caesar's soldiers, intimidated them:

> To all right-thinking people it seemed a fantastic thing that those who were getting so much from Caesar should be urging the Senate to give him money, as though he had none. Though "urge" is not the right word. It was rather a question of compulsion, and the Senate groaned at the decrees for which it voted. . . . Some were overawed by Pompey and Crassus, and nearly everyone wanted to please Caesar. So they [the senators] did nothing [to upset Caesar], living in hopes of future kindnesses from him.[30]

And so, no Roman dignitary dared to object publicly to Caesar's plans for new military campaigns. These were to extend from northern Illyricum into the rugged German lands of central Europe. But these plans were cut short when, soon after the meeting at Luca, he received news of new trouble in Gaul. After his conquests of the central and northern parts of the region, Roman traders and officials began visiting distant fringe areas inhabited by peoples who had not yet dealt directly with the Romans. Among these peoples were the Veneti, a maritime tribe with a powerful fleet of ships, who lived on the Atlantic shores of Brittany. When Roman officers demanded that the Veneti supply them with grain, the tribal leaders refused and took the officers as hostages. The Veneti decided to make a stand against Rome and their trading partners, the Britons, from across the nearby English Channel, offered their support.

Fearing that the rebellion might spread to other parts of Gaul, Caesar hurriedly prepared to march on the Veneti. At first he was irritated and angry at this unexpected crisis. But his mood improved as he considered that Brittany was the gateway to the mysterious island of Britain. Well before he reached Veneti territory, his mind was filled with visions of British tin and pearls.

Chapter

4 Land of the Unexpected: Caesar's Adventures in Britain

The second phase of Caesar's Gallic conquests, lasting from late 56 to late 54 B.C., involved preparing and executing his invasion of the then remote island of Britain. Though it was separated from the European mainland by the English Channel, which varied in width from twenty to one hundred miles, Caesar viewed Britain as, in a sense, part of Gaul. This was mainly because of the heritage of those who inhabited the fabled "island of tin." Most of the Britons were Celts, who were closely related to and in regular contact with the Celts in Gaul.

In addition to this cultural link between island and mainland, Caesar had a number of what he considered compelling reasons for invading Britain. The first was at last to afford the Romans firsthand knowledge of this mysterious land on the edge of the known world. Secondly, and much more importantly, Caesar wanted to exploit Britain's legendary natural resources, which, besides tin, supposedly included gold, silver, iron, cattle, corn, and pearls. Thirdly, a successful invasion of Britain was sure to bring Caesar much personal wealth, glory, and prestige. In addition, there were two more immediate and strategic reasons for opposing the Britons. First, a number of Belgian tribesmen who remained hostile to Caesar had

taken refuge in Britain, which they planned to use as an anti-Roman base. Second, the Britons themselves were giving aid to the Veneti, who were presently in open rebellion against Rome.

A warrior of ancient Britain, equipped with battle-ax, shield, and short spear. The Britons, like the Gauls, hailed from Celtic stock.

Hulls of Solid Oak

Caesar realized that he first had to deal with these rebellious Veneti before any invasion of Britain could be launched from their territory of Brittany. And his Gallic informants had convinced him that subduing the tribe would not be easy. As Caesar recorded in his journal:

> These Veneti are much the most powerful people in all this part of the coast. They have the biggest fleet in the area and are in the habit of sailing to and from Britain. In the theory and practice of navigation they are superior to all the other [Gallic] tribes. They live on a stretch of open sea which is particularly rough, and as they themselves control the few harbors that exist, they are able to impose taxes on almost all vessels that normally sail in these waters.[31]

The Veneti's main advantage was the excellent construction of their ships. Caesar had given orders for a fleet of Roman warships to be built in western Gaul and sailed up the coast toward Brittany. But these vessels, like other Roman ships, were better suited to the calmer waters of the Mediterranean. By contrast, the hulls of the Veneti warships were made of solid oak planks fastened with thick iron bolts. Though not as fast as the Roman ships, these heavier vessels could better withstand the impact of both Atlantic storms and Roman rams.

Another distinctive feature of the Veneti ships turned out to be a severe strategic disadvantage. This was the fact that they used sails exclusively, while the Roman ships also employed oars. Caesar's naval commanders, led by the young but capable Decimus Brutus Albinus, devised a clever way to exploit the Veneti's total reliance on sails. The Romans fashioned large, sharp hooks and secured them on the ends of long poles. The plan was to move alongside a Veneti ship, extend the poles, and use the hooks to snap off the rigging supporting the enemy sails. With-

A fleet of Roman war galleys, called triremes. Each such ship typically carried over a hundred soldiers and could reach a ramming speed of twelve miles per hour.

out their sails and having no oars, the Veneti vessels would be incapable of maneuvering and thus would be wide open to a boarding by Roman legionnaires. This plan worked exceedingly well when the opposing fleets met in the autumn of 56 B.C. near Quiberon Bay, on the coast of Brittany. According to Caesar's eyewitness account, once his men put the enemy's sails out of commission,

> all that was left was a contest . . . [of] sheer fighting ability, and in this our soldiers were easily the superior, especially as this battle was fought under my own eyes and those of the whole [land] army, so that every particular gallant piece of fighting was bound to be noticed. Our troops occupied the cliffs and the high ground from which one could get a good view of the sea. Once the yardarms [sail supports] of an enemy ship had collapsed . . . two or three of our ships would come alongside and our soldiers would vie with one another in storming their way aboard. . . . We pursued and boarded their ships one by one, with the result that only a very few out of their whole fleet managed, when night came on, to get to shore. The battle had lasted from 10 A.M. until sunset.[32]

With their fleet, the backbone of their defense, devastated, the Veneti wasted no time in surrendering to Caesar. If they expected that he would show them mercy, they were mistaken, for he intended to make them an example. "I decided that they should be treated severely," he wrote, "so that in future the natives should be taught to respect more carefully the laws respecting the rights of envoys."[33] After executing all of the tribal leaders, Caesar sold the rest of the population into slavery. Like the Nervii, the Veneti abruptly and tragically disappeared from the pages of history.

Bridge on the River Rhine

Having all of Brittany now under his firm control, Caesar began making preparations for the invasion of Britain. These plans were of necessity long-range, for winter was setting in, making the Atlantic waters too cold, stormy, and dangerous to risk a channel crossing. It would be better, Caesar reasoned, to wait until late spring or early summer, when it was safer. So he once more traveled south and spent the winter months in Cisalpine Gaul. There he spent many a night questioning the few Gallic traders he could find who had been to Britain. He hoped that any information they could give him, however sketchy, would aid him in drawing his invasion plans.

In the early spring of 55 B.C., eager to launch his British campaign, Caesar headed north through the thawing alpine passes. But once more he encountered a delay. It was another migration of Germans across the Rhine, this time by two large tribes, the Usipetes and the Tencteri. The Rhine frontier had remained quiet for almost three years, and Caesar was determined to keep it that way. Marshaling several legions, he intercepted the migrating Germans near the junction of the Rhine and Moselle Rivers in northeastern Gaul. As the Romans approached the vast sea of men, women, children, animals, and wagons—a horde larger even than that of the Helvetii—the Germans pan-

A Structure Adapted to Nature's Forces

The fifteen-hundred-foot-long trestle type of bridge that Caesar's men constructed across the Rhine River in 55 B.C. was a typical example of the large-scale engineering projects for which the Romans were famous. According to Caesar's own account in his Commentaries, *the bridge followed this plan.*

"Two piles, eighteen inches thick, slightly pointed at the lower ends and of lengths varying in accordance with the depth of the river, were fastened together two feet apart; they were then lowered into the river from rafts, fixed firmly in the river-bed, and driven home with piledrivers [machines consisting of heavy weights maneuvered up and down by pulley systems]. Instead of being driven in vertically, as piles usually are, they were fixed obliquely [at an angle], leaning in the direction of the current. Opposite these . . . and forty feet downstream, another pair of piles was fixed and coupled together in the same way, though this time they were slanted forward against the force of the current. The two pairs of piles were then joined by a beam, two feet wide, the ends of which fitted exactly into the spaces between the two piles of each pair. The pairs were kept apart from each other by braces which secured each pile to the end of the cross-beam. The piles were thus both held apart and, in a different sense, clamped together. The whole structure was strong and so adapted to the forces of nature that the greater the strength of the current, the more tightly locked were the timbers."

icked, turned, and fled headlong for the rivers. "I sent the cavalry after them to hunt them down," Caesar recalled.

The Germans heard the noise of shouting behind their backs and could see how their own people were being slaughtered. They threw away their arms . . . [and] when they reached the confluence of the Moselle and the Rhine, they saw that there was no hope of escaping further. Great numbers were killed and the rest hurled themselves into the river and perished there, overcome by panic, exhaustion, and the force of the current.[34]

Once more exaggerating a death toll, Caesar estimated that 430,000 of the enemy had died. The real figure was perhaps one-fifth of that, which was still a tragic slaughter. Considering that not a single Roman lost his life, it was also a victory of epic proportions, although "victory" is perhaps an inaccurate term, since no formal battle took place.

A group of Germanic tribesmen crosses the Rhine River on a log raft. Caesar dazzled the natives by building a huge bridge over the river, allowing his own soldiers to cross more quickly and easily.

To discourage any more German intrusions into Gaul, Caesar stayed an extra month at the Rhine before moving westward toward the English Channel. He ordered his men to build a wooden bridge fifteen hundred feet long and forty feet wide, across the river. He then crossed over with part of his army and for eighteen days marched his men in a conspicuous display through German territory. With this intimidating gesture of psychological warfare, he served notice to those natives who watched at a distance that he could easily invade their country whenever he pleased. "I wanted the Germans," he wrote, "to begin to have some worries of their own, as they would when they realized that a Roman army had both the daring and the ability to make the crossing."[35] Leaving behind a contingent of troops to guard the Rhine frontier, he then crossed back into Gaul and hurried toward the Atlantic coast.

In mid-July 55 B.C. Caesar gathered his invasion forces in the coastal village of Gesoriacum, now Boulogne, at the north-ern tip of France. He had assembled just eighty ships and only two legions, no more than twelve thousand men, for his first foray into the Britons' little-known island kingdom. His decision to take so few troops was partly strategic in nature. He planned to invade in two stages, the purpose of this initial stage being to establish a beachhead, or foothold, and base of operations in southern Britain. Once he had a chance to evaluate the nature of the country and the size and quality of the British defenses, he would leave and return later with reinforcements.

Fighters for Caesar's Glory

Another reason Caesar took along such a small initial force was the outstanding quality of his own soldiers. After three years of campaigning with him in Gaul, his men now constituted a tough, highly trained, and steadfastly loyal fighting force that he believed could overcome any soldiers in the world. One way he had built so fine an army was through the stirring personal example he set. Caesar never demanded that his men should do or endure anything that he himself would not. According to Suetonius, he was

> highly skilled in arms and horsemanship, and of incredible powers of endurance. On the march he headed his army, sometimes on horseback, but oftener on foot, bareheaded both in the heat of the sun and in rain. He covered great distances with incredible speed . . . very often arriving before the messengers sent to announce his coming.[36]

Caesar wisely employed a number of other means of raising his soldiers' morale and grooming them into a crack professional fighting force fiercely loyal to him alone. He made camp life more ordered and efficient and also doubled the men's pay, raising the huge revenue needed through his contacts in Rome, including the wealthy and influential Crassus. In addition, Caesar took a keen and apparently sincere interest in his soldiers' personal needs and problems, often touring his camp and engaging in long and spirited one-on-one conversations. It was not surprising, then, that Caesar was able, as Plutarch wrote,

> to secure the affection of his men and to get the best out of them. . . . Soldiers who in other campaigns had not shown themselves to be any better than the average became irresistible and invincible and ready to confront any danger, once it was a question of fighting for Caesar's honor and glory.[37]

With soldiers like these, men who looked on Caesar's camp as a homeland more sacred than Italy itself, Caesar reasoned that two legions would be sufficient to intimidate the disorganized barbarians he expected to meet in Britain.

A Native Welcoming Committee

However, for the first and what would prove to be the only time in his long military career, Caesar had underestimated an opponent. The Britons, though politically and militarily less advanced than the Romans, were highly organized on the tribal level and possessed a number of effective military tools, including cavalry and war chariots. Moreover, the Britons were proud, courageous, and willing to fight to preserve their traditional ways. They had received regular reports from their brethren on the mainland about the impending invasion. Thus, as the Romans' ships approached the white cliffs rising behind the beaches at what is now Dover in southeastern England, an unexpected "welcoming committee" awaited. Caesar wrote:

> I myself, with the leading ships, reached Britain about 9 A.M. We could see the enemy's armed forces lined up all along the cliffs. At this point there was a narrow beach with high hills behind it, so that it was possible to hurl weapons down from the higher ground onto the shore. It seemed to me an extremely bad place to effect a landing, and so we waited at anchor until about three-thirty P.M. for the rest of the ships to join us. . . . The signal was given to weigh anchor and, af-

Thrust Rather than Slash

The Roman legionnaire's most lethal weapon was his two-foot-long sword. In his book Warriors of Rome, *scholar Michael Simkins explains that the way in which these swords were used was the key to their effectiveness.*

"The method taught was to thrust, rather than to slash at an opponent; for a slash-cut rarely kills, but a thrust makes a deep penetration of the vital organs. The Roman short sword was clearly designed for stabbing, with its sharp angled point, though it could be . . . used to effect cutting strokes. The skulls belonging to the hapless defenders of the great Durotrigian fortress . . . in Dorset, England [one of the British strongholds the Romans assaulted], show the appalling fatal wounds inflicted by [Roman legionnaires] against adversaries who were most probably unhelmeted."

ter moving on about eight miles, we ran the ships ashore on an open, evenly shelved beach.[38]

But the move to a different landing spot had not eliminated the danger of attack. The hordes of British warriors followed the ships along the coast and stood ready to fight on the beaches as the first vessels approached the shore. The Romans experienced several disadvantages at first. Most of the legionnaires had to jump in and wade ashore through cold heavy surf, a task for which their training in the warmer, calmer Mediterranean waters had not prepared them. Their armor and weapons weighed them down and slowed their advance, giving the enemy defenders ample opportunity to shower them with spears and rocks. Also, the Romans could go ashore only a few at a time. According to Caesar, when the British warriors "saw from the beach any part of our men disembarking one by one from a ship, they

spurred their horses into the water and attacked while we were at a disadvantage and they could swarm around a few of us at a time in superior numbers."[39]

Eventually, the Romans were able to push back the assault and establish a beachhead. Under normal circumstances Caesar would next have sent his cavalry in pursuit of the retreating enemy and thereby gain control of territory well inland from the beach. But the ships carrying his cavalry, perhaps hampered by strong currents and tides in the channel, had not yet arrived. While waiting for these reinforcements, Caesar was surprised to see a delegation of natives approaching. The British envoys, apparently impressed by and fearful of the Roman soldiers, claimed that they now wanted peaceful relations with Caesar. This timid display turned out to be only a trick to buy time. The leaders of the coastal tribes had already sent messengers inland to rally other tribes against the invaders. Caesar discovered the ruse the hard way when he sent out small groups of men to forage for food, a necessity since most of the army's supplies were on the cavalry transports. Bands of Britons attacked the foragers, some of whom Caesar rescued after seeing a distant dust cloud and recognizing it as a sign of attacking horsemen.

Caesar soon encountered further unexpected difficulties. Four days after the initial landing, the cavalry transports finally appeared on the horizon. But before they could land, Caesar later recalled,

> such a violent storm arose that none of [the ships] could hold course. Some were carried back to the harbor from which they had set out; others, at

great peril to themselves, were swept southward toward the westerly part of the island. In spite of the danger they dropped anchor, but began to ship [take on] so much water that they were forced to put out to sea again in the darkness and make for the Continent [mainland].[40]

Making matters worse, the storm, along with unusually high Atlantic tides, damaged or waterlogged many of the ships near the beachhead. Caesar was left without either cavalry reinforcements or sufficient supplies just as new and increasingly severe native attacks on the Roman position began. There seemed no choice but to abandon the project, and at the first sign of fair weather he ordered a return to northern Gaul.

The Roman D Day

Caesar was not used to failure and refused to recognize the aborted invasion as such. In his *Commentaries* he glossed over what amounted to his forced retreat to the mainland, claiming he believed it safer to sail now, in summer, than to wait and "risk sailing in wintry weather." Dismayed at experiencing unexpected resistance and natural disaster rather than what he described as "my usual good luck," he was now more determined than ever to conquer the Britons.[41] For the first time since beginning his Gallic campaigns, he did not travel south to spend the winter in Cisalpine Gaul. Instead, he remained in Transalpine Gaul and supervised preparations for a much larger foray against Britain. Roman-controlled ports all over Gaul and as far away as Spain received orders to build ships

Caesar's legionnaires wade ashore to face the fierce half-naked Britons in the first Roman invasion of Britain.

Roman troop transports crowd the English Channel during Caesar's second invasion of Britain. The more than eight hundred vessels carried over twenty thousand men, plus horses, weapons, and supplies.

and troop transports. By the spring of 54 B.C., Caesar was able to assemble over eight hundred vessels, containing five legions and two thousand horsemen, the largest invasion force the channel would see until World War II's famed D day invasion nearly two millennia later.

After more unexpected delays, in June Caesar's formidable armada approached the British coast, and this time the Romans encountered no opposition at all. Caesar concluded that the sight of his huge fleet had frightened the enemy off. But this was not the case. The coastal tribes had already wisely decided to move inland and, along with other local tribes, to place themselves under a single powerful commander. He was Cassivellaunus, who ruled over the region centered at what is now Saint Albans, a few miles north of the Thames River and London. Cassivellaunus planned to lure the Romans away from their coastal base into wild and heavily wooded territory that his own fighters knew well. There he would lay ambushes for the invaders.

The decisive encounter that both Caesar and the British leader anticipated was delayed, however. No sooner had Caesar begun to march his troops inland when messengers caught up with him and described how another severe gale had just wrecked much of the fleet. Caesar hurried back to the coast and, as he recorded in his journal,

> Saw with my own eyes that the situation was almost exactly as it had been described to me by the messengers. . . . About forty ships were a total loss; but it seemed that it would be possible to repair the rest, though this would mean much hard work. I therefore picked out from the legions all soldiers who were skilled craftsmen and sent instructions for others to be brought over from the Continent. . . . I decided that, in spite of the enormous labor involved, the best thing to be done was to have all the ships beached. . . . We spent about ten days in getting this done, the work going on continuously day and night.[42]

When he was satisfied that the rebuilding effort was going smoothly, Caesar set out again to accomplish his main goal—to subdue the Britons. But the natives were determined to thwart his plans. Once the Romans were well inland, Cassivellaunus began launching effective guerrilla warfare tactics with which the legionnaires, used to more formal, organized battles, were unfamiliar. The British chariots would careen out of the woods late in the day just as the Romans were setting up camp. Two or three armed warriors would jump off each chariot, spar with bands of Roman defenders, and then jump back aboard the vehicles, which would speed away into the cover of the darkening forest. The Britons relentlessly continued these tactics, denying Caesar the formal, pitched battle in which he knew his men would have the advantage.

Caesar finally gained his advantage, although not through the large battle he desired. As a secret weapon he had brought along an Indian elephant, which for weeks he had kept well concealed. He was sure that the locals had never seen or even heard of elephants and that they would likely be terrified by it. As his troops approached the Thames, the Britons waited and watched from the woods on the far side of the river. Suddenly Caesar's men unleashed the huge beast and, sure enough, the natives panicked and fled.

The British Charioteers

The Greeks and Romans used chariots for transportation and sports racing but not for war. Therefore, Caesar's legionnaires were taken off guard when the Britons used chariots against them. In his Commentaries, *Caesar offered this description of the havoc the British chariots caused.*

"The tactics employed by these charioteers are as follows: First they drive in every direction, hurling their spears. Very often the sheer terror inspired by the galloping horses and the noise of the wheels throws their opponents into a state of confusion. They then make their way through the squadrons of their own cavalry, leap down from the chariots, and fight on foot. Meanwhile the drivers retire a little from the battle and halt the chariots in a suitable position, so that if those who are now fighting on foot are hard pressed by the enemy, they will have an easy means of retreating to their own lines. So in their battles they combine the mobility of cavalry with the stamina of infantry. Daily training and practice have brought them to a remarkable state of efficiency. They are able, for example, to control their horses at full gallop on the steepest slopes, to pull them up [slow them down] and turn them in a moment, to run along the pole [connecting the vehicle to the horses], stand on the yoke, and dart back again into the chariot."

Caesar then advanced into Cassivellaunus's homeland and ravaged the countryside. Wary now of the Romans, several of the tribes withdrew their support from Cassivellaunus, who eventually had no choice but to send an envoy to ask Caesar for peace terms.

The Losses Outweigh the Gains

If Caesar's acceptance of the surrender and his subsequent brief occupation of Cassivellaunus's fortress at Saint Albans constituted a Roman victory, it was a hollow one. With only a small fraction of southern Britain under his control, Caesar was forced once more to withdraw from British lands. Autumn was setting in, and the cold, stormy weather it would surely bring would pose a new danger to the fragile fleet. Also, there was not enough time before winter to set up the large supply train that would be needed to support further campaigns inland. In addition, reports were arriving daily telling of increased unrest among the Belgian tribes of Gaul.

For these reasons Caesar once more felt compelled to halt his conquest of what had turned out to be a land of seemingly endless unexpected difficulties. In order to make his small gains seem more impressive to people back in Rome, he demanded that Cassivellaunus provide him with hostages and pay the Romans tribute in the form of gold and other valuables. These moves did not fool Caesar's political adversaries, however. His longtime opponent, the well-known senator Marcus Cicero, for example, complained that Caesar had gotten nothing of value from his

The British chieftain Cassivellaunus surrenders to Caesar in 54 B.C. However, Caesar's gains in Britain were meager.

British invasion. Despite the legends, said Cicero, it was now clear that Britain had no substantial supplies of silver. Moreover, the amounts of British gold and jewels Caesar had sent to Rome were meager. Caesar's expensive expeditions, Cicero declared, held out "no hope for booty other than captives, among whom I believe you cannot expect any highly qualified in literature and music [at which captives from Greece and other lands excelled]."[43]

Though he did not say so publicly, Caesar must have realized that Cicero was right. The expedition's losses had far outweighed its gains. The plain fact was that Caesar's adventures in Britain had been his only military campaign that had not ended an unqualified success. He would soon find, however, that new adventures awaited him in Gaul, where he would manage to score the large-scale and lasting triumphs the fierce and stubborn Britons had denied him.

Chapter

5 Native Wrath and Roman Steel: The Great Gallic Rebellion

After abandoning Britain a second time, Caesar landed at his base in Gesoriacum in the autumn of 54 B.C. His mood was somber for two reasons. First, news had recently arrived that his only child, Julia, the wife of his fellow triumvir, Pompey, had died in childbirth. The baby boy, Pompey's son and Caesar's grandson, had died, too. Caesar's political adversaries in Italy and elsewhere had high hopes that this loss of a close personal tie between himself and Pompey might weaken the triumvirate.

The other bad news was that unrest was brewing among the Belgae in northern Gaul. When Caesar had first taken control of the region, the native tribes appeared to be pacified. But that had been before the arrival of a steady stream of Roman tax collectors, businessmen, and slave

Roman legionnaires with a group of Gallic prisoners during Caesar's long, relentless campaign to subdue Gaul.

buyers. The onslaught of the Romanization process provided the Belgian tribes with a rude awakening, one experienced by their cousins all over Gaul. It was the sober realization that the old Gallic way of life was about to end, perhaps forever.

More and more Gauls came to the conclusion that the only way to save their traditional society was to rise up and throw out the Romans. Those Gauls who had helped and sympathized with the Romans were also targets of native wrath. The first serious result of that wrath, an episode that occurred shortly after Caesar returned from Britain, was the murder of the leader of the Carnutes, who inhabited north-central Gaul. Because Caesar had personally chosen the man as local chief, the assassination was clearly an insult and a warning aimed directly at the Roman leader. Only a few weeks later the Belgae took the more daring step of overt attacks on Roman military units.

Caesar feared that these incidents might be only a foretaste of a much larger Gallic rebellion. And that fear would be realized. In the following three years, in what would prove to be the third and last phase of his Gallic conquests, he would lead new and vigorous campaigns in the region. In crushing native resistance for good, he would sound the death knell for the old Gaul and vault himself to new pinnacles of military and political power.

They Fell Where They Stood

That Caesar foresaw the possibility of widespread trouble in northern Gaul is clear from his actions after hearing of the Carnute chief's murder. He decided to di-

Like all Roman military camps, this one erected by Sabinus and Cotta at Aduatuca had a secure wooden stockade.

vide his forces into small armies of one or two legions each and station them in potential trouble spots throughout the countryside. Among the commanders of these units were Caesar's able assistants Gaius Fabius, Quintus Cicero, Lucius Roscius, and Titus Labienus. In addition to these veteran legions, Caesar had about a legion and a half of new recruits recently raised in the northern reaches of Cisalpine Gaul. He ordered this unit, under the command of Quintus Sabinus and Lucius Cotta, to guard the Eburones, a Belgian tribe inhabiting the rugged lands stretching between the Rhine and Meuse Rivers.

It was this untried military unit, the weakest link in Caesar's northern defensive chain, that encountered the first large-scale violent outburst. With winter setting in, Sabinus and Cotta ordered their force, numbering more than seven

A cameo captures the likeness of Quintus Sabinus, a commander in Caesar's army. Lacking experience, Sabinus made errors in judgment that helped cause the massacre of his own forces.

thousand, to make camp at a place the natives called Aduatuca. The Eburones, led by their chief, Ambiorix, suddenly attacked the camp. But the assault had little effect since, like all Roman army encampments, the enclosure was surrounded by a secure wooden stockade and was well defended. Undeterred, that night the cunning Ambiorix managed to lure the inexperienced Sabinus and his troops out of the camp and into a deadly ambush. According to Caesar, the Gauls waited in the dark woods

> for the Romans to arrive, and, when the greater part of our force had descended into a deep ravine, they suddenly appeared at both ends of the

column, falling upon the rear guard and trying to prevent the men in front from climbing out of the ravine. . . . At this point Sabinus, who up to now had no idea that such a thing could happen . . . hurried around, trying to get the troops into position; but even this he did nervously, making it obvious that he had completely lost control of the situation. . . . Cotta, on the other hand, had thought that something like this might happen on the march and had therefore been against leaving the camp. Now he did everything possible to save the army, leading and encouraging the men like a good general, and fighting in the line like a good soldier.[44]

But Cotta's efforts were in vain. After several hours of fighting, Ambiorix called for a short truce and a conference, and Sabinus, disregarding Cotta's objections, agreed. As soon as Sabinus and his assistants were well behind the enemy line, Ambiorix ordered them slain. Then, as Caesar told it:

> The natives at once raised their customary cry of triumph and, yelling and screaming, charged down upon our army and broke through the ranks. Cotta fell fighting where he stood and most of the troops died with him. The remainder retreated to the camp from which they had set out. . . . Since there was no hope left, every man of them committed suicide. A few soldiers had managed to slip away while the fighting was going on. By taking roundabout routes through the forests they succeeded in reaching Labienus's camp [to the south, in Remi territory] and told him what had happened.[45]

Caesar's Vengeance

The news of the massacre at Aduatuca spread quickly through the Roman ranks and within a few days reached Italy. There the public reaction was lament for the dead. In private many people questioned Caesar's judgment in sending raw recruits into such a potentially dangerous situation. Indeed, this first large-scale loss of Roman troops in his Gallic campaign was clearly an embarrassment for Caesar. It was also personally upsetting for him, for he deeply cared about all the men under his command. Filled with anger and grief, he abandoned his usual clean-cut grooming habits and let his hair and beard grow, swearing never to cut them until he had avenged the victims of the massacre.

The Gauls received the news of the massacre in a decidedly different way. Already unhappy with Roman rule and contemplating resistance, many tribes were elated and encouraged at hearing that Caesar's forces were not, as they had seemed for so long, invincible. The spirit of rebellion swiftly spread from one tribe to another. It soon reached Samarobriva (modern Amiens) about three hundred miles southwest of Aduatuca, where Quintus Cicero was camped with his legion, a total of no more than six thousand men. An army of perhaps sixty thousand Gauls suddenly surrounded Cicero's well-fortified position, which, unlike his unfortunate colleague Sabinus, he was wise enough not to abandon. Several savage assaults, some aided by crude siege towers the Gauls had modeled after those of the Romans, hammered the camp. The besieged Romans, steadfastly maintaining their discipline and organization, man-

aged to hold out until Caesar himself rescued them. Wrote Plutarch:

> Cicero's camp was very nearly taken by storm, and every man in it was wounded in the course of the most gallant defense against what seemed to be impossible odds. Caesar was far on his way [to another location] when he heard the news of what had happened. He turned back at once, got together 7,000 men in all, and hurried to the relief of Cicero. The besiegers, however, got to know of his approach and, feeling nothing but contempt for his small force, came out to meet him and destroy him. Caesar, playing on their overconfidence, kept on avoiding battle. . . . He kept his soldiers from making any attacks on the enemy, and made them act as though they were afraid. . . . This strategy had the effect of making the enemy despise him all the more, until the time came that their confidence led them to make a disorderly attack. . . . Caesar then led his men out, and routed the enemy, killing great numbers of them.[46]

While this battle raged, Titus Labienus, encamped several miles to the east, also came under siege. He managed to fend off the attackers only after killing their chief.

Caesar wanted to discourage any further such incidents. To this end, early in 53 B.C. he ordered all the Gallic chieftains to meet him at Samarobriva. Representatives of the Carnutes and several other tribes did not attend, which amounted to an act of open defiance. Caesar then called for another meeting a hundred miles to the south at Lutetia (modern Paris), where he demanded that all tribes submit to

"An Extremely Great Stroke of Luck"

Caesar was determined to pursue and punish Ambiorix, the Eburone chief who had wiped out the Roman garrison commanded by Quintus Sabinus and Lucius Cotta. In this excerpt from his Commentaries, *Caesar described the events and outcome of the pursuit.*

"As soon as the crops began to ripen, I set out myself on the campaign against Ambiorix, marching through the forest of the Ardennes, which is the largest forest in Gaul . . . and is more than five hundred miles long. I sent Lucius Minucius Basilus with all of the cavalry in front of the main army, hoping that by advancing quickly he might get a chance of doing something valuable. I ordered him not to allow any fires in his camp, so that the enemy could not get warning of his approach . . . and told him that I should be following him directly. Basilus carried out these instructions and completed his march much more quickly than most people thought possible. He took the natives by surprise, captured a number of them in the fields, and acting on information received from them, made directly for Ambiorix himself in the place where he was reported to be with only a small cavalry escort. In war, as in everything else, fortune plays a very great part. Basilus was extremely lucky in catching Ambiorix completely off his guard and unprepared. . . . But it was by an extremely great stroke of luck that Ambiorix himself escaped with his life, after losing all the military equipment he had with him, including his carriages and horses. . . . The house where he stayed was in the middle of a wood, as is usual among the Gauls, who generally build their houses near woods and streams in order to avoid the heat. Fighting in a confined space, his friends and followers managed for a short time to hold up the attack of our cavalry. While this fighting was in progress, one of Ambiorix's men mounted him on a horse and he escaped under cover of the woods."

Roman domination. Most of the Gauls in attendance, convinced that it would be unwise to kindle Caesar's wrath further, agreed. A few did not, and Caesar now turned on these with a brutal vengeance.

He marched on the Eburones, who had initiated the rebellion by massacring Sabinus's force, and wiped out the tribe without mercy. Other defiant tribes soon felt the killing touch of Roman steel. To set a final example, in the autumn of 53 Caesar assembled all of the Gallic leaders. While they watched, he had Acco, chief of the rebellious Senones tribe, stripped naked, bound to a stake, beaten to death, and finally beheaded. Satisfied that he had at last avenged his massacred men, Caesar calmly cut his hair and shaved.

A Grand Insurrection

Caesar's harsh treatment of the rebels had the desired effect, for a bitter but quiet lull fell over Transalpine Gaul. Believing that he had crushed the resistance, the Roman leader journeyed south and spent the winter of 53–52 B.C. in the warmer and more pleasant pastures of the Po Valley. But he soon learned that the resistance in Gaul, far from being crushed, was alive and well and building toward another outburst. Rebel leaders had taken heart by news of recent events in Italy and beyond. In the summer of 53 Marcus Crassus had died while leading a military expedition of his own in the eastern reaches of the empire. And in Rome, with Caesar's daughter barely cold in the grave, Pompey married the daughter of Metellus Scipio, an aristocrat who supported the Senate and disliked Caesar.

With the triumvirate seemingly in ruins, many Gallic leaders sensed that Caesar's power base in Rome was crumbling. This, they reasoned, might be their only reasonable opportunity to throw off the Roman yoke once and for all. As Ernle Bradford explains:

Even the favored tribes knew that they would never enjoy real freedom again

A Gallic tribal chief. Despite being tough, courageous fighters, the Gauls lacked unity, effective military organization, and long-range planning.

and, in Caesar's absence, the mood began to harden throughout Gaul. It was clear that individual uprisings were of no avail and that only a massive insurrection on a *national* scale (something never previously envisaged) could secure them their liberty.[47]

Early in 52 most of the central region of Transalpine Gaul exploded in a grand insurrection. The first violent incident, as in the previous uprising, occurred among the Carnutes, who suddenly seized and executed a number of Roman citizens in the town of Cenabum. As Caesar recorded in his journal:

The Carnutes, led by two thoroughly abandoned [disreputable] characters called Cotuatus and Conconnetodumnus, at a given signal made a sudden descent on Cenabum, where they massacred all Roman citizens who had

One of the several later and romantic artistic renditions of the Arverni chieftain Vercingetorix appearing before Caesar in a Roman stronghold.

settled there as traders and plundered their property. Among those killed was Gaius Fufius Cita, a distinguished Roman knight, whom I had put in charge of the grain supply. The news spread quickly through all the states of Gaul. In fact when anything happens in Gaul that is particularly important or remarkable, the people shout out the news from one to another across the whole extent of the country; each takes up the report in turn and passes it on to his nearest neighbor. So it happened in this case. What had taken place in Cenabum at dawn was known before eight P.M. in the country of the Arverni, about one hundred fifty miles away.[48]

Learning of the Carnutes' bold actions, dozens of other neighboring tribes followed their lead and rebelled. Almost immediately the Arverni, whose homeland stretched between those of the Carnutes and Aedui, assumed leadership of the rebels. For years the Arverni had been one of the most powerful tribes in Gaul. But they had been too preoccupied with nearly constant squabbles among their own leaders to offer the Romans any organized resistance. Now under the leadership of a strong new war chief, Vercingetorix, the Arverni finally focused their considerable energies and hostilities on the Roman occupiers.

Vercingetorix had earlier been a member of Caesar's Gallic cavalry, a unit of friendly natives he had used to supplement his core of Roman horsemen. Having fought alongside the Romans, Vercingetorix was familiar with Roman tactics and weaknesses. He was also intelligent, shrewd, and undoubtedly the most talented military leader that ancient Gaul ever produced. According to Caesar, the Arverni leader called

> upon his countrymen to take up arms in the cause of the liberty of Gaul, [and] soon got together large forces. . . . He was proclaimed king by his followers. Messengers were sent out in every direction urging other tribes to stand by him, and in a very short time he had acquired the support of the Senones, Parisii, Pictones, Cadurci, Turoni, Auleric, Lemovice, Andes, and [many] other tribes. . . . By general consent he was given supreme command. With this power in his hands, Vercingetorix demanded hostages from all the above-mentioned states [to ensure their loyalty], ordered each of them to send to him at once a fixed number of troops, and assigned the quantity of arms which had to be got ready in each state before a certain time. He paid particular attention to his cavalry. He combined very great efficiency with extreme strictness of discipline, and the sever-

ity of his punishments had the effect of bringing over the waverers [those unsure about joining him] to his side. Serious crimes were punished by death at the stake [being burned alive] or under all kinds of torture; in the case of slighter offenses, the criminal was sent home with his ears cut off or one eye gouged out, to serve as a lesson to the rest. . . . By such savage means as these he soon got an army together.[49]

Upon hearing of these events, Caesar hurried northeastward through the Alps. Winter still lingered in the mountains and the main traversable pass, which ran through the Cervennes (now Cévennes) peaks, was choked with over six feet of snow. But Caesar did not allow this obstacle to stop his usual swift and decisive offensive. He ordered thousands of troops to shovel a path, and in only a few days he reached Arverni territory. Perhaps at this juncture he foresaw defeating Vercingetorix, who appeared to be just the latest in a series of insolent Gallic upstarts, as a relatively easy task. But the tough and cunning Vercingetorix was determined to make the Romans pay in blood for every inch of territory they seized. Caesar had no way of knowing that an ordeal more difficult and dangerous than any he had yet faced in Gaul was about to begin.

6 Scorched Earth and Siege Works: Caesar Victorious

It is not difficult to understand why, after nearly two thousand years, the nineteenth- and twentieth-century French erected statues to honor the heroism of their ancestor, the Gallic chieftain Vercingetorix. Though he was ultimately unsuccessful in his attempt to stop the Romans, he accomplished a feat that no one else duplicated before or after him. This was to fight Julius Caesar, one of the greatest military generals in history, to a standstill. Had the stubborn Gallic leader possessed a better-trained army and supply trains to match those of the Romans, he might have kept his mighty opponent at bay for years. As it was, Vercingetorix cost the Romans many lives and much precious time and showed them that the conquest of Gaul would not come cheap. His defense of his homeland marked Gaul's last great stand against the nearly irresistible onslaught of Roman imperialism.

A Deadly Contest

The first phase of Vercingetorix's defensive strategy took his opponent by surprise. Caesar had hurried through the Alps, expecting to gather his troops and march into battle. Arriving in Arverni territory early in 52 B.C., he quickly assembled nearly eight legions and marched on the enemy, hoping to force them into a formal, pitched battle, the kind of fighting that favored the Romans. But Vercingetorix, knowing better than to allow Caesar to exploit Roman strengths, wisely retreated. This was part of an overall strategy designed to weaken the Romans. Like his adversary, the clever Gaul understood the importance of supply trains in maintaining large armies on the march. Planning to deny the Romans the opportunity to capture and live off the considerable supplies of grain and livestock the Arverni had recently accumulated, Vercingetorix instituted a "scorched-earth" policy. In his journal, Caesar explained why and how this was executed, saying that the Gauls planned

> to do everything possible to cut the Romans off from forage and supplies. . . . Since the safety of everyone was at stake, individuals must give up their rights to their own property; all villages and farm buildings must be set on fire on each side of the Roman line of march to the distance within possible reach of their foragers. . . . The Romans . . . would either starve or be forced to take the great risk of marching a long way from [the defensive se-

Caesar Frustrated

An excellent example of Vercingetorix's grasp of military affairs was the way in which he continually kept Caesar guessing about what the Gauls would do next. This excerpt from Caesar's journal describes one of the many frustrating and uncertain moments he experienced as a result of his wily opponent's unexpected tactics.

"After reaching the winter camp, I sent messengers to the other legions and had them all concentrated in one place before it was possible for the Arverni even to have heard that I had got there. When he did receive the news, Vercingetorix led his army back again into the country of the Bituriges and went on from there to attack Gorgobina, a town of the Boii, whom I had settled there under Aeduan protection after their defeat in the battle I fought with the Helvetii. This move of Vercingetorix made it very difficult for me to decide what to do next. If I kept all the legions together for the rest of the winter, a people supposedly under Aeduan protection might be overpowered and all the rest of Gaul, thinking that I was incapable of bringing help to my friends, might join in the revolt. On the other hand, if I led the army out of winter quarters too early in the year, difficulties of transport might give us serious trouble with regard to our grain supply."

curity of] their camp. . . . Finally, all towns which were not so well fortified . . . as to be safe from any danger ought to be set on fire; otherwise they might be used by . . . the Romans, who would plunder their supplies. And if, Vercingetorix concluded, these measures seemed cruel and difficult to bear, [his followers] should consider how much worse than all this it would be to have their wives and children carried off as slaves and to be killed themselves—which would certainly happen if they were conquered.[50]

Most of the "towns" that Vercingetorix advocated destroying were *oppida*, the mas-

sive hill forts so common in Gaul, especially in the southern and central regions. The Gallic leader had been right in his fears that Caesar would assault these forts to capture their supply stores. Among Caesar's initial moves were sieges of the *oppida* at Cenabum and Vallaunodunum, both in north-central Gaul. Vercingetorix subsequently burned dozens of *oppida* in an effort to rob the Romans of any more such prizes. At the same time Vercingetorix himself laid siege to the main *oppidum* of the Boii, one of the few tribes that remained Roman allies. The assault served two purposes—to punish the tribe and to deny Caesar its support. Thus, the first stage in the war between Caesar and his

Gallic opponent amounted to a deadly contest to see who could control or destroy the most *oppida*.

A Heroic Defense

Perhaps the most dramatic episode in this tragic contest involved the *oppidum* of Avaricum, now Bourges in central France, the main settlement of the Bituriges, who inhabited the region directly west of the Loire River in central Gaul. As Caesar's legions approached, about forty thousand people from the surrounding villages and farms fled behind the fort's massive walls. In the ensuing siege the Bituriges put up a heroic defense.

Despite their bravery the unfortunate residents of Avaricum were up against invaders who were experts in capturing fortified towns. The Romans were among the most skilled of all ancient peoples in the art and science of conducting sieges. A typical Roman siege began with the army surrounding the town or fort to be captured. To make sure that none of the besieged could escape, the legionnaires usually dug a pit around the town and filled the pit with water, creating a moat. Another common tactic was to dig holes and fill them with sharp wooden stakes or metal spikes. Enemy soldiers who stumbled into such pits were impaled, almost always with fatal results. Earthen ramparts four to ten feet high sometimes ran for thousands of feet or even several miles around the town. These were usually a feature of long sieges, in which the Romans wanted to keep the besieged tightly contained and to starve them into submission.

During actual attacks on a besieged town, the Romans employed a number of means. To approach a wall without suffering injury from enemy arrows, rocks, and other missiles, they formed a testudo, or turtle. This consisted of a group of soldiers who covered themselves completely with a mass of shields and moved in tight

The Romans use a testudo-like formation of massed shields to move horses and equipment across a muddy obstacle.

Roman siege works in action. A large stationary crossbow rests in the right foreground while soldiers employ a battering ram against a fortification at left.

unison. The legionnaires also fired spears, often with flaming tips, into the town from large, stationary crossbows. Or they used an onager, a heavy catapult that could hurl huge rocks almost a third of a mile. Once they had softened the enemy defenses with these methods, the Romans used various ladders and scaffoldings to breach the defensive walls. Or they brought up their siege towers, rectangular wooden structures that stood as high as or higher than the walls. Some soldiers huddled inside the towers while others pushed them up to the walls. At the right moment a drawbridge dropped from the summit of each tower, and the soldiers swarmed over the wall and into the town.

The Romans followed these standard procedures in their siege of Avaricum. But the courageous and clever defenders fought back with every means they could devise. Caesar, who respected a worthy opponent, recorded some of these means, writing in his *Commentaries:*

> Our men showed the most remarkable courage and energy, but were confronted by all sorts of contrivances [schemes] on the part of the Gauls, who were indeed a most ingenious race, wonderful imitators, and very good at making practical use of ideas suggested to them by others. For example, they lassoed our siege hooks and, when they had caught them fast, pulled them aside and hauled them into the town by means of windlasses [cylinders turned by cranks]; they also

tried to undermine our ramp and did this remarkably skillfully, for they do a lot of iron mining in their country and know all about the various methods of working underground. Moreover, they had built towers all along the whole circuit of their wall and covered them with hides. They were constantly making sorties [attacks] by both day and night and either trying to set fire to our ramp or attacking the men who were working on it. And as our ramp rose day by day and our towers came up higher, they correspondingly raised the level of their own towers by building on extra stories. They also countermined our subterranean [underground] tunnels and tried to prevent their extension to the wall by making fences of fire-hardened stakes, by pouring in boiling pitch, or by blocking the way with enormous stones.[51]

In the end, however, the Bituriges' heroic efforts were in vain. The persistent and indignant Caesar eventually took the town and ordered a brutal massacre, from which only about eight hundred of the forty thousand inhabitants managed to escape.

Vercingetorix's Fatal Blunder

But not all of Caesar's efforts were so successful. In a similar attack on the Arvernian *oppidum* of Gergovia, he found the fort too strong to overcome without a prolonged siege, which he lacked the time and resources to pursue. And after so many years as a Roman ally, the powerful Aedui tribe finally turned on Caesar and joined its Gallic brethren. Because of in-

creasing Roman difficulties, Vercingetorix had a real chance to seize the advantage. Had he continued with his scorched-earth policy, he might have forced Caesar to come to terms favorable to the Gauls or at least delayed a Roman victory for several years. But Vercingetorix, having grown overconfident, eventually made the fatal blunder of engaging his opponent in open battle. The Gaul suddenly ordered a massive cavalry charge on the Roman army. Though the battle was hard fought on both sides, Caesar's troops prevailed, and the Gauls had to retreat.

Vercingetorix quickly fell back with about eighty thousand men to the main Arverni stronghold, the huge *oppidum* at Alesia, about two hundred miles east of Avaricum. According to Caesar:

The actual fortress of Alesia was on the top of a very high hill and appeared to be impregnable [unconquerable] except by blockade. Rivers flowed along the bottom of the hill on two sides. In front of the town there was a plain about three miles long. Everywhere else it was closely surrounded by hills which were about the same height as that on which the town itself stood. The whole of the eastern slope of the hill below the town wall was filled with Gallic troops, who had fortified their camp with a ditch and a six-foot wall.[52]

Immediately after his soldiers had surrounded the Alesia fortress, Caesar ordered them to erect siege works. Describing these, which were far more massive, complicated, and deadly than those at Avaricum, Anthony King writes:

The inner ditch [moat] of the siege-works was filled with water from the

Trenches and Battlements

This passage from Caesar's Commentaries *is just part of his own long and detailed description of the siege works erected around the Arverni stronghold of Alesia.*

"I dug a trench twenty feet across; the sides were perpendicular, so that it was just as wide at the bottom as at the top. All the other siegeworks were set back about 650 yards behind this trench. This was because our lines had necessarily to cover a very large area and the whole circuit could scarcely be manned by a continuous chain of troops. I therefore wanted to guard against any sudden night attack that the enemy might launch en masse against our fortifications, and I also wanted to prevent them from shooting [arrows] during the day at our men when they were at work. Behind the 650-yard interval I dug two trenches, fifteen feet broad and of the same depth, all the way around. The one nearer the town ran across ground that was level with or below the level of the plain and I had it filled with water diverted from the river. Behind the trenches a rampart with palisades [fences] twelve feet high was erected; this was strengthened by a breastwork [earthen wall] with battlements; below this, at a point where it joined the rampart, large forked branches projected outward to prevent the enemy from climbing up. Towers were erected at intervals of about 130 yards all around the whole circuit of fortifications."

This drawing of the Roman siege works surrounding the Gallic fortress of Alesia was reconstructed from Caesar's own descriptions.

streams . . . and behind it were fields of barbed iron spikes (*stimuli*) and sharpened stakes (*cippi*) set in the ground, together with half-hidden foot-traps with sharpened stakes in them (*lilia*). Behind these . . . were two more ditches and the rampart [defensive wall], further protected by entanglements of branches. The rampart had . . . towers at frequent intervals, plus redoubts [fortified enclosures] for detachments from the legions. These redoubts and various larger [fortified] camps behind the siegeworks were . . . protected by an outer rampart some fourteen miles long which enclosed the whole of Caesar's army.[53]

This huge and complex project was completed in less than thirty days by almost fifty thousand men laboring day and night. The Gauls who watched from behind Alesia's ramparts must have been struck with awe and fear at the fantastic scope of Roman organization and engineering skill.

Caesar's strategy of enclosing his siege works by an outer rampart clearly showed that he anticipated the arrival of a Gallic force to relieve Alesia. Sure enough, nearly two months into the siege a huge Gallic army approached. The size of this force is difficult to determine, but it included contingents from forty-three tribes and could have numbered as many as 100,000 to 150,000 warriors. Evidently, Caesar wrote, the Gauls

> thought that the mere sight of their enormous host would prove too much for us, especially as we were to be attacked from two directions at once, and would have to face a sortie [attack] from the Gauls inside Alesia [as well as] the huge mass of cavalry and infantry of their relief force.[54]

Just as Caesar had foreseen, Vercingetorix saw in the arrival of the new Gallic force his chance to break out of besieged Alesia. He began launching attacks from the inside of the siege works just as the relief army started its own assaults from the outside. For four tumultuous days Caesar, greatly outnumbered, led a brilliant defense against almost relentless waves of attackers from all sides. Finally, at noon on the fourth day, Caesar personally led a daring charge against the main contingent of the Gallic relief army. As he described it:

> The enemy could see that I was coming because of the scarlet cloak which I always wore to mark me out in action. And as the lower slopes along which I came were visible from the higher ground, they could also see the squadrons of cavalry and the cohorts [troop units] which I had ordered to follow me. So the enemy rushed into battle. The shout [war cry] was raised on both sides. . . . Our men dispensed with spears and got to work with their swords. Suddenly the Gauls saw our cavalry coming in from the rear; fresh cohorts [of Roman infantry] were also bearing down. The enemy turned and ran. As they ran, the cavalry were upon them. There was a great slaughter.[55]

An Impressive but Tragic Record

Caesar's sudden and overwhelming victory against seemingly impossible odds

Another later artistic version of the Gallic leader Vercingetorix surrendering to Caesar after the fall of the Alesia fortress.

completely shattered the morale of the surviving Gauls. They swiftly abandoned their huge camp, fled into the countryside, and eventually returned to their respective lands. Seeing all hope lost, Vercingetorix surrendered. Thus, with the fall of Alesia the great Gallic rebellion largely collapsed. A few tribes, most notably the Bituriges and some of the Belgae, continued to resist and forced Caesar to carry on his campaign for another year. But this resistance was both disorganized and futile. Caesar easily destroyed these tribes one by one, and by the end of 51 B.C. his conquest of Transalpine Gaul was at last complete.

In his nearly eight years in Gaul and Britain, Caesar had fought over thirty major battles, captured more than eight hundred towns, and killed over a million people. To the Romans this was an impressive record. For the Gauls it was a tragic and despicable one. In the end they had lost not from a lack of bravery, determination, or willingness to sacrifice, but because the Romans were more organized and experienced in the art of war.

The Gauls had had the additional misfortune of facing one of the most talented generals of all time, a brilliant strategist and an inspiring leader. Indeed, it was Caesar's ability to bring out the very best

Caesar addresses his troops. Caesar's close bond with his soldiers contributed greatly to his success as a general.

of them responded with emotion. The strength of this magnetic bond emerges in a thousand ways from [the pages of] the *Commentaries*. . . . One of the finest orators of the day, he addressed his men continually and effectively. He shared their hardships and their perils.[56]

This magnetic bond between commander and soldiers, backed up by superior Roman weapons, supplies, and military organization, was simply too much for the old, disunited Gallic society to deal with.

As Caesar headed south for the fertile fields of the Po Valley, from where he would later move on to Rome and new military adventures, he left behind a civilization forever altered. Within mere weeks of his departure, a new Roman army was on its way to Gaul. This one was composed of traders, merchants, and money lenders; of teachers, artists, and architects; of lawyers, administrators, and slave dealers. Whether for good or ill, and in spite of their fears and protests, the Gauls were about to experience profound and lasting change. The Roman tidal wave that had already engulfed the Mediterranean world had finally reached their shores.

in his soldiers that was his greatest asset. As Michael Grant puts it:

> To the ordinary legionnaires, he was bound fast in a brilliantly successful relationship to which almost every one

7 The Wheel of Destiny: Rome's Legacy in Gaul and Britain

Caesar's conquest of Gaul extended Rome's Mediterranean empire well northward into Europe. This had two important consequences, one immediate and the other long-term. The immediate effect of the Roman absorption of Gaul was its enrichment of the empire. Gaul's considerable farmlands, metal ores, trade networks, and human resources vastly increased Rome's wealth and power. Gallic plenty helped Roman leaders in the following two centuries to maintain prosperity and to continue expanding the empire's borders. Even after these borders eventually began to shrink, Gaul remained an important and valuable asset. In time it became so completely Romanized that few of its residents could imagine how it could ever have been independent and fiercely anti-Roman.

The long-term effect of Gaul's Romanization, and of Britain's, too, occurred after Rome declined and ceased to be a great power. Over the centuries many new kingdoms and nations grew up in the lands that had once been Roman provinces. But though Rome no longer controlled these lands, its influence remained in the form of the potent cultural legacy it bequeathed them. Roman language, customs, laws, and political ideas profoundly shaped the lives of later Mediterranean and European peo-

ples, including those in what had once been Gaul and Britain. The modern nations of France, Belgium, and Britain, which today occupy former Gallic and Celtic soil, owe much to Rome's legacy. "Rome yet lives in France, to which it gave its language, its spirit, and the traditions of

A later European drawing of a triumphant Caesar in ceremonial garb and wearing a crown of laurel leaves.

its thought," remarked classical scholar Guglielmo Ferrero.[57] Clearly then, though Caesar died long ago, the effects of his conquests can still be detected in the very fabric of modern Europe.

Caesar's Later Conquests

Caesar himself did not foresee the decline of Rome and other such sweeping changes. Like most other Romans of his day, he envisioned that Rome was an eternal concept in the minds of the gods and, therefore, that it would rule the world forever. The key factor in that rule, of course, was naked power. And he certainly believed that he was destined to play a pivotal role in shaping Roman power. After all, attaining great military and political power for himself had been the primary goal of his Gallic campaigns.

Caesar succeeded in achieving this goal, to a degree perhaps beyond even his own high expectations. In 50 B.C., with his Gallic conquests complete, he camped with his army in Cisalpine Gaul and contemplated how best to take control of Rome. At that moment the capital was in turmoil. The triumvirate was in shambles, and while Pompey, the consuls, and the Senate each vied for authority, they all feared facing Caesar's military might. In a feeble attempt to remove Caesar's fangs, the Senate ordered him to lay down command of his army. When he did not, the legislature relieved him of his proconsulship. He was left with the choice of going along with this decree, and thereby giving up the power he had worked so long and hard to acquire, or defying the government, and thereby igniting a civil war. On January 10, 49 B.C., Caesar made his fateful choice. He paused with his troops at the Rubicon River, the recognized border between his province and the Italian heartland. According to Suetonius:

> Realizing what a step he was taking, he turned to those about him and said, "Even yet we may turn back; but once we cross that little bridge . . . the whole issue is with the sword.". . . Then Caesar cried "Take we the course which the signs of the gods and the false dealing of our foes point out. The die is cast."[58]

With these words, Caesar led his men across the river and plunged the Roman world into tragic civil strife.

The devastating war that pitted Roman brother against brother and father against son lasted over four years. Pompey and many senators fled Italy and raised an army in Greece. There, on August 9, 48 B.C., on the plain of Pharsalus, in east-central Greece, Caesar's army of forty-five thousand met the senatorial forces, which were nearly twice as numerous. Despite the odds Caesar won an overwhelming victory. In the following months and years, Caesar went on to defeat other armies raised by a number of adversaries. His legions waged battles from Egypt to the Far East, from Africa to Spain, and always they were triumphant. The only fighting in Gaul was on the southern coast. After the independent Greek city of Massalia came out against Caesar, he captured it, and thereafter it was just another Roman Gallic town. With the civil war at last over, Caesar entered Rome in September 45 as the undisputed master of the Roman world and quite literally the most powerful human being who had ever lived.

Caesar leads his army across the Rubicon River, the recognized border between his province of Cisalpine Gaul and Italy proper, and thereby plunges the Roman world into a devastating civil war.

Caesar had big plans for the empire, including Gaul. He wanted all parts of the Roman realm to reach new heights of prosperity and for all Romans, regardless of social status, to benefit from it. This would be good for both the people and the state. The best way to keep the Gauls at peace and under control, for example, was to make them citizens and give them better, more comfortable lives. And he firmly believed that the best way to achieve peace and increased prosperity was by abandoning many of the old republican ways and placing most state power in the hands of a benevolent dictator, namely himself. He took on the task of "reshaping the Roman state," as James Breasted puts it,

> a task in which the Roman Senate had so completely failed. . . . Caesar did not abolish the ancient body, but he greatly increased its numbers, filled it with his own friends and adherents

[supporters], and even installed former slaves and foreigners among its members. He thus destroyed the public respect for it, and it was entirely ready to do his bidding. The new Senate could not obstruct him, and hence the whole . . . administration of the provinces centered in him. . . . In all this he was launching the Roman Empire. He was, in fact, its first emperor [though not in name], and only his untimely death continued the death struggles of the Republic for fifteen years more.[59]

The Egypt of the West

The instrument of Caesar's death was a group of veteran senators who feared that Caesar's dictatorship would spell the end of the Roman Republic. They stabbed him to death in the Senate on March 15, 44 B.C. But this rash act did not save their beloved republic. It only plunged the empire into another ruinous civil war, in which new military strongmen emerged to compete for ultimate power. Caesar's grandnephew, Gaius Octavius, known as Octavian, emerged victorious and established the same sort of benevolent dictatorship his uncle had envisioned. In 27 B.C. Octavian took the unprecedented title of Imperator Caesar Augustus, "The Great Victor and Ruler." He then enjoyed a long and relatively peaceful reign as the first true emperor in the autocratic state that

A statue of Octavian in his new, self-imposed role as Caesar Augustus, "first citizen" of Rome, and in reality the first Roman emperor.

came to be known as the Roman Empire.

Gaul remained an important part of the new Rome. Augustus, as the emperor was called, realized that Gallic lands could provide the empire with vast and valuable natural resources. Twenty years after Caesar's conquests Gallic production of wheat and flax alone was already nearly as large as that of Egypt, which had previously been Rome's primary source of these goods. "Gaul seems to have been the sole region of Europe fertile enough to be able to export grain," explained Ferrero,

> to have been for Rome a kind of Canada or [American] Mid-west [huge grain producers] of the time, set not beyond oceans but beyond the Alps. . . . Augustus was first to recognize . . . [that Gaul] was producing grain like Egypt, linen like Egypt, that the arts of civilization for which Egypt was so rich and famous were beginning to prosper there. Augustus was not the [kind of] man to let slip so tremendous a piece of good luck. . . . He found finally the grand climax of his career, to make Gaul the Egypt of the West, the province of the greatest revenues in Europe.[60]

Just as importantly, Gaul could be used as a base of operations from which an emperor could, if he chose, launch new conquests into Germanic central Europe. It was, therefore, important to keep the process of Romanizing Gaul going. Part of this process involved keeping Gaul and the memory of Caesar's conquests there alive in the public's mind. Gaul needed to be an ever present and attractive option for Roman settlers and investors. Augustus therefore provided plenty of funds for the *Ludi Victoriae Caesaris.* Instituted when Caesar was alive, this was a public holiday celebrated from July 20 to July 30 to observe Caesar's Gallic victories.

The Three Gauls

An even more important part of the Romanization process was the physical reorganization of the Gallic territories and introduction of Roman culture. In 27 B.C., only months after assuming his new imperial titles, Augustus visited Gaul. He formally announced that henceforth the region would consist of four Roman provinces. The nearly century-old Narbonese in the south was retained. The rest of what had been Transalpine Gaul became the provinces of Aquitania, encompassing the southwest and west-central regions; Lugdunensis, stretching from the northwest coast into the east-central lands; and Belgica, in the northeast. These three new provinces became known collectively both as the Tres Gallia, "Three Gauls," and Gallia Comata, or "Long-haired Gaul," a reference to the

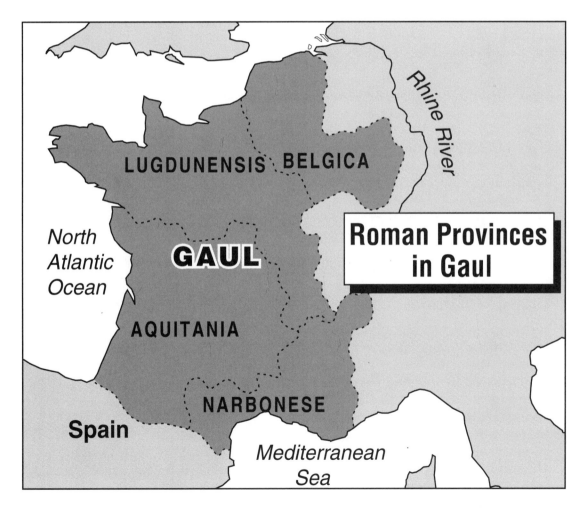

native men's traditional shoulder-length hair.

Augustus and his successors built roads, aqueducts, and public buildings in the new Gallic provinces, and for the first time real cities grew in these lands. Local industries expanded, especially the growing of olives and grapes. The lasting influence of the Romans in this respect is illustrated by the fact that modern France is still renowned for is fine grapes and wines. The Roman timber industry also expanded north from the Narbonese. Some Gauls became master weavers, others invented new ways to dye cloth, and still others became renowned for their silver- and tin-plating processes. According to the ancient Roman scholar Pliny the Elder:

> They cover the copper with tin in such a way that it is difficult to distinguish it from silver. It is a Gallic invention. Later they began to do the same thing with silver, silver-plating especially the ornaments of horses and carriages. The merit of the invention belongs to the Bituriges [tribe], and the industry was developed in the city of Alesia. After the same fashion there has been spread everywhere a foolish profusion [vast number] of objects not only silver-, but gold-plated. All of this amounts to the worship of elegance![61]

In addition, a number of Gauls learned to read and write Latin. And over time a somewhat distorted version of Latin largely replaced the old Celtic tongues in conversation as well. Most Gauls came to accept common Roman ideas and customs, just as Roman roads and laws came to bind the once wild and remote Gallic fields and forests to the older, more refined Mediterranean cultures.

Roman Britain

Even more remote and wild than Gaul, Britain also became a target of Roman exploitation. Caesar had failed to conquer or absorb the island to any significant extent, and his legionnaires were the last Romans to visit it for over a century. Augustus and his great-grandson, the third Roman emperor, Gaius Caesar, known as Caligula, each seriously considered a new invasion of Britain. But because of pressing problems in Italy and other parts of the empire, neither actually launched such an operation.

The task finally fell to the fourth emperor, Claudius, Caligula's uncle. In A.D. 43 Claudius's capable general, Aulus Plautius,

The emperor Claudius, portrayed inaccurately with European-style mustache and clothes in a later fanciful painting.

No Match for the Legions

In this excerpt from his article "Roman Britain," in the Oxford Illustrated History of Britain, *historian Peter Salway compares the Roman and British forces who fought each other during the invasion launched by the emperor Claudius.*

"The force assembled to sail to Britain in A.D. 43 comprised four legions and about the same number of auxiliary troops, around 40,000 men in all. Facing this disciplined machine, the British forces retained their old character [as in Caesar's day]. The permanent warriors were the aristocracy; their favorite weapon was the chariot, which they used for rapid transport in and out of battle and in the handling of which their drivers were extremely skilled. The exact status of the cavalry is uncertain: they were probably men who could provide their own horses, but it is not clear that their prime occupation in life was fighting. The mass of the British armies were the levies [draftees] summoned from the farms. Unlike the armored Romans, the Britons wore little or no body protection and depended on speed . . . and the long slashing sword. Before they could get near to Romans in battle order [formation] they were liable to lose many men to the clouds of Roman javelins [spears]; and in hand-to-hand combat their long blades were at a disadvantage faced with the closed ranks and short stabbing swords of the enemy infantry. Successes by these Celtic troops against the Romans were usually gained in surprise attacks, in ambushes, and when overwhelming detached [isolated] units by sheer numbers. They could rarely match the legions in pitched battle."

sailed with an army of forty thousand troops from Gesoriacum, the same port from which Caesar had embarked. Plautius swept aside what little resistance he encountered and quickly seized control of Britain's southeast region. Claudius himself soon made the journey to the island to ensure that he would get the credit and prestige for leading the invasion. He stayed less than four weeks, during which he accepted the surrender of several British chiefs at Camulodunum (modern Colchester) near the southeast coast. Then he returned to Rome and left Plautius and others to continue the subjugation of the country.

In the following three to four years, most of the southern and central regions of Britain fell under Roman control, and the island became the newest of Rome's provinces. For the Britons the blow of losing their freedom was softened some-what by the lenient nature of Roman provincial rule. Although the Roman governor had the final say on important matters, the locals were allowed largely to manage their own affairs. According to scholar Peter Salway:

> Roman practice in the provinces was always to shift as much of the burden of administration on to the loyal locals as soon as might be. The Claudian intention seems to have been to employ [local] "client" kings as far as possible—the most economical method, where they were reliable. A substantial part of the south . . . was put in the hands of one Cogidubnus [a local leader]. . . . One success of this policy was . . . the enduring loyalty of Cogidubnus, which was almost certainly of critical importance during later crises in Britain. The rest of the province the governor would expect to administer chiefly through the tribes, reorganized as Roman local government units (*civitates*) with their nobles formed into councils. . . . In addition, throughout the province ran the writ [authority] of the chief financial secretary of Britain, the *procurator provinciae*. These local provincial procurators reported directly to the emperor.[62]

While the southern and central regions of Britain underwent Romanization, the Romans continued their conquests in the more mountainous and remote western and northern regions. By 84 nearly all of the island, including what is now southern Scotland, came under Rome's sway. Roman Britain then largely prospered for another three centuries until the empire began to fall apart in the early 400s.

Waves of Barbarians

Rome's decline had a direct and crucial effect on the later development of both Britain and Gaul. Already weakened by more than a century of poor leadership, civil disorders, and severe economic problems, in the early fifth century Rome faced its greatest challenge yet. The Huns, a savage, nomadic central-Asian people, swept into Europe, driving other Asian and European peoples westward before them. Among the displaced groups, often referred to as "barbarians," were the Goths and Vandals. The Goths split into two groups, the first of which entered Gaul and displaced many of the natives, who fled southward. The second group, known as the Visigoths, headed into Italy and sacked Rome in 410. A few years later the Vandals moved into Gaul, burning, pillaging, and displacing more natives, and the even more destructive Huns, under their fierce war leader Attila, soon followed. Attila ravaged Gaul until a combined army of Romans and Visigoths, both of whom feared and hated him, defeated him in a huge battle in 451.

But the removal of the Hunnish menace did little to improve the situation in Gaul, Rome, or anywhere else in western Europe. In 476 the last Roman emperor vacated the throne, and Rome's control and influence over Gaul, Britain, and its other former provinces, already nearly nonexistent, ceased altogether. Restless Germanic tribes, including the Franks and Burgundians, overran Gaul. And Britain once more became a remote, seldom visited island. In general western Europe sank into a virtual dark age of fear, cruelty, murder, civil disorder, and despair. As the noted scholar Charles Van Doren describes it:

> Western Europe, once so tightly held together, had simply fallen apart. Where once great social and economic organization had existed, there were now hundreds of small communities. The Roman Empire had been an open world, with a single language, Latin, that was understood everywhere; with a single code of law that everyone obeyed; with good roads that joined its far-flung regions. . . . Now . . . the roads were mostly empty of travelers and freight, people spoke different languages and few could read, and there was little law except that of force. In the century between about 450 and 550 A.D. . . . most of the openness disappeared. . . . Those hundred years . . . were among the most terrible periods in Western history. . . . At the end of this period of rapine and death the region now called Europe was utterly changed.[63]

A Bountiful Harvest

The new Europe that emerged from the Roman Empire's wreckage was a disorderly patchwork of weak and culturally backward kingdoms. Some of them encompassed considerable territory, but many were no larger than a single town and its surrounding villages and farmlands. Under the control of powerful local lords and kings, these kingdoms fought among themselves and variously rose, fell, and merged.

It was through this process that France and England developed. In the Gallic lands once ruled by the Belgae, the Frankish kings emerged victorious and then expanded their rule over all of former Roman Gaul. And in Britain, the Germanic Saxons and Angles, who had invaded the island in the late 400s, merged with the local Britons to form the Anglo-Saxon culture. In 1066 the Normans, descendants of the Franks, invaded Britain and conquered the Anglo-Saxons. From the resulting blended culture grew the

The "barbarian" Franks cross the Rhine River into Gaul. Their name would eventually be preserved in the name of France, the modern nation that would one day rise from the wreckage of the fallen Gallic kingdoms.

William the Conqueror lands his Norman forces in southern Britain in 1066, one of the most decisive events of European history.

distinctive language and customs of the English people. By the year 1300 the former Roman Gaul and Britain had developed the basic cultural identities of the modern nations of France and England. These countries subsequently became two of the most powerful in Europe and went on to colonize and control vast portions of the globe.

During all of this turbulent cultural evolution, old Roman roads still linked many of the cities in each nation. France and England also retained many Roman laws and judicial ideas that profoundly influenced their developing governments as well as the everyday lives of their peoples. The legacy of the Latin language was equally large. Gaul's own peculiar variation of Latin evolved into modern French, while Latin combined with French and early Anglo-Saxon German to produce modern English.

The development of French, one of the "Romance" languages along with Spanish, Portuguese, and others, illustrates this process. When Caesar conquered Gaul in the first century B.C., most of the local natives spoke a Celtic tongue called Gaulish. After the conquests, as the Gauls became increasingly Romanized, they adopted Latin, not the formal version written and spoken by educated Romans. Gallic Latin was a vulgarized, or common, form of the language characterized by the odd pronunciations that derived from native accents and by numerous slurrings and other changes in everyday Latin speech.

For example, in formal Latin the word *bonitatem*, meaning "kindness," was pronounced with stresses on the syllables *bon* and *ta*. The Gauls isolated these sounds and ran them together, changing the word to *bonta*, which eventually became *bonté* in French. As French continued to develop, it retained a few old Gaulish words, along with some German words contributed by the Franks and some Greek words left over from the influence of traders from the Greek city of Massalia.

In the 900s the emerging French language split into two distinct dialects. The one used mainly in the north, near the growing city of Paris, a version known as the *langue d'oil*, eventually became the language spoken all over France. Between 1300 and 1550 many new Greek, Latin, Italian, and Spanish words and expressions entered French, and finally, in the 1600s, scholars standardized the language's grammar and vocabulary. Since that time French has undergone only minimal change.

Thus, ironically, Rome acted as both destroyer and creator. Though the Romans devastated the original Celtic cul-

Migrating Germans

In this excerpt from his lecture "The Germans and Their Wanderings," collected with others in The Invasion of Europe by the Barbarians, *the late British historian J. B. Bury discussed the backgrounds of some of the Germanic "Barbarians" who migrated through western Europe in the last years of the Roman Empire.*

"The events of the fifth century were decisive for the future of Europe. The general result of these events was the occupation of the western half of the Roman Empire, from Britain to North Africa, by German peoples. Now the Germans who effected this occupation were not, with one or two exceptions, the Germans who had been known to Rome in the days of Caesar and Tacitus [the second-century A.D. Roman historian]. They were not West Germans. They were East Germans. The principal of the East German peoples were the Goths, the Vandals, the Gepids, the Burgundians, and the Lombards. There were also the Rugians, the Heruls, the Bastarnae, the Sciri. Most of [the descendants of] these peoples believed that they had reached the [Baltic] coast of East Germany from Scandinavia, and this tradition is confirmed by the evidence of names. The best students of German antiquity [ancient history] identify the name of the Goths with that of the Scandinavian Gauts. The Rugians are explained by Rogaland in Norway. . . . Of these East German peoples, most were moving slowly through Europe in a generally southward direction, to the Black Sea and the Danube [River], in the third and fourth centuries. . . . The earliest great recorded migration of an East German people was that of the Goths, about the end of the second century. They moved from their homes on the lower Vistula [River, in what is now Poland] to the shores of the Black Sea, where we find them in A.D. 214."

tures of Gaul and Britain, in doing so they gave birth to new, different, and ultimately successful European cultures. "The wheel of destiny," Guglielmo Ferrero remarked, "turns by a mysterious law, alike for families and for peoples: those in high position may fall; those in low, may rise."[64]

Under the tread of Caesar's legions, Gaul fell. Yet it eventually rose to become a nation as great as or greater than the one that had nurtured its conqueror. And in this way time and human determination transformed the bleak and bitter seeds of Caesar's conquest into a bountiful harvest.

Notes

Introduction: The Vista of a New World

1. Suetonius, *Lives of the Twelve Caesars*, translated by J. C. Rolfe. Cambridge, MA: Harvard University Press, 1964.

2. Michael Grant, *Caesar*. London: Weidenfeld and Nicolson, 1974.

3. Ernle Bradford, *Julius Caesar: The Pursuit of Power*. New York: William Morrow, 1984.

Chapter 1: An Ancient Kinship Lost: Urban Rome Versus Rural Gaul

4. James Henry Breasted, *Ancient Times: A History of the Early World*. Boston: Ginn, 1944.

5. Breasted, *Ancient Times*.

6. Donald R. Dudley, *The Romans, 850 B.C.–A.D. 337*. New York: Knopf, 1970.

7. Anthony King, *Roman Gaul and Germany*. Berkeley: University of California Press, 1990.

8. J. F. C. Fuller, *Julius Caesar: Man, Soldier, and Tyrant*. New Brunswick, NJ: Rutgers University Press, 1965.

9. Chester G. Starr, *The Ancient Romans*. New York: Oxford University Press, 1971.

10. Julius Caesar, *Commentaries on the Gallic Wars*, in *War Commentaries of Caesar*, translated by Rex Warner. New York: New American Library, 1960.

11. Plutarch, *Life of Caesar*, in *Lives of the Noble Grecians and Romans*, excerpted in *Plutarch: Fall of the Roman Republic*, translated by Rex Warner. Baltimore: Penguin Books, 1958.

12. Suetonius, *Lives of the Twelve Caesars*.

Chapter 2: Caesar the Imperialist: The Beginning of Old Gaul's End

13. Breasted, *Ancient Times*.

14. Lily Ross Taylor, *Party Politics in the Age of Caesar*. Berkeley: University of California Press, 1968.

15. Caesar, *Commentaries*.

16. Caesar, *Commentaries*.

17. Caesar, *Commentaries*.

18. Fuller, *Julius Caesar*.

Chapter 3: Gaul's Savage Frontiers: The Peace of the Sword Descends

19. Caesar, *Commentaries*.

20. Caesar, *Commentaries*.

21. Plutarch, *Life of Caesar*.

22. Caesar, *Commentaries*.

23. Caesar, *Commentaries*.

24. Caesar, *Commentaries*.

25. Caesar, *Commentaries*.

26. Bradford, *Julius Caesar*.

27. Caesar, *Commentaries*.

28. Caesar, *Commentaries*.

29. Caesar, *Commentaries*.

30. Plutarch, *Life of Caesar*.

Chapter 4: Land of the Unexpected: Caesar's Adventures in Britain

31. Caesar, *Commentaries*.

32. Caesar, *Commentaries*.

33. Caesar, *Commentaries*.

34. Caesar, *Commentaries*.

35. Caesar, *Commentaries*.

36. Suetonius, *Lives of the Twelve Caesars*.

37. Plutarch, *Life of Caesar*.

38. Caesar, *Commentaries*.

39. Caesar, *Commentaries*.

40. Caesar, *Commentaries*.

41. Caesar, *Commentaries*.

42. Caesar, *Commentaries*.

43. Cicero, *Letters to Atticus*, translated by E. O. Winstedt. Cambridge, MA: Harvard University Press, 1961.

Chapter 5: Native Wrath and Roman Steel: The Great Gallic Rebellion

44. Caesar, *Commentaries.*
45. Caesar, *Commentaries.*
46. Plutarch, *Life of Caesar.*
47. Bradford, *Julius Caesar.*
48. Caesar, *Commentaries.*
49. Caesar, *Commentaries.*

Chapter 6: Scorched Earth and Siege Works: Caesar Victorious

50. Caesar, *Commentaries.*
51. Caesar, *Commentaries.*
52. Caesar, *Commentaries.*
53. King, *Roman Gaul and Germany.*
54. Caesar, *Commentaries.*
55. Caesar, *Commentaries.*
56. Grant, *Caesar.*

Chapter 7: The Wheel of Destiny: Rome's Legacy in Gaul and Britain

57. Guglielmo Ferrero, *Characters and Events of Roman History, from Caesar to Nero,* translated by Frances L. Ferrero. New York: G. P. Putnam's Sons, 1909.
58. Suetonius, *Lives of the Twelve Caesars.*
59. Breasted, *Ancient Times.*
60. Ferrero, *Characters and Events.*
61. Quoted in Ferrero, *Characters and Events.*
62. Peter Salway, "Roman Britain," in Kenneth O. Morgan, ed., *The Oxford Illustrated History of Britain.* New York: Oxford University Press, 1986.
63. Charles Van Doren, *A History of Knowledge: The Pivotal Events, People, and Achievements of World History.* New York: Ballantine Books, 1991.
64. Ferrero, *Characters and Events.*

For Further Reading

Julius Caesar, *The Battle for Gaul*, translated by Anne Wiseman and Peter Wiseman. London: Chatto and Windus, 1980. This recent translation of Caesar's famous journal, *Commentaries on the Gallic Wars*, is contemporary, easy to read, and accompanied by several illustrative drawings and photos.

Lionel Casson, *Daily Life in Ancient Rome*. New York: American Heritage Publishing, 1975. A fascinating presentation of how the Romans lived: their homes, entertainments, eating habits, theaters, religion, slaves, marriage customs, government, and more.

Peter David, *Julius Caesar*. New York: Crowell-Collier Press, 1968. A good general synopsis of Caesar's life, including his campaigns in Gaul. Written for basic readers.

G. B. Harrison, *Julius Caesar in Shakespeare, Shaw, and the Ancients*. New York: Harcourt, Brace and World, 1960. This extremely useful volume is a grab bag of works by and about Caesar, including Shakespeare's *Julius Caesar*, Shaw's *Caesar and Cleopatra*, Suetonius's *Lives of the Twelve Caesars*, Plutarch's biographies of Caesar, Brutus, and Mark Antony (all three from the 1579 Sir Thomas North translation), and excerpts from Cicero's letters and Caesar's own Gallic commentaries. Much of this is advanced reading for young people but is definitely worth the effort. Highly recommended.

Anthony Marks and Graham Tingay, *The Romans*. London: Usborne Publishing, 1990. A summary of Roman history, life, customs, and military and political figures. Written for basic readers and illustrated with hundreds of beautiful, accurate, color drawings.

Don Nardo, *Cleopatra* and *Julius Caesar*. San Diego: Lucent Books, 1994 and 1996. In what can be considered companion volumes to this discussion of Caesar in Gaul, the author presents more extensive information about the famed leader's life, including his rise to power, the triumvirate, his campaigns in Greece, Africa, and Spain, and his relationship with the Egyptian queen.

———, *The Roman Republic* and *The Roman Empire*. San Diego: Lucent Books, 1994; *Greek and Roman Theater*. Lucent Books, 1995; *The Battle of Zama* and *The Punic Wars*. Lucent Books, 1996. In these concise summaries of Rome's rise to power, its culture and religion, and its eventual decline, the author provides background material and a context for understanding Caesar and the forces that shaped him.

Chester G. Starr, *The Ancient Romans*. New York: Oxford University Press, 1971. An easy-to-read general survey of Roman history, with a number of informative sidebars on such subjects as the Etruscans, Roman law, and the Roman army. Also contains many primary-source quotations by ancient Roman and Greek writers.

Works Consulted

Appian, *Roman History*, translated by Horace White. Cambridge, MA: Harvard University Press, 1964. This is an invaluable primary source that describes in great detail the late republic, the civil wars, and the exploits of the powerful men, including Caesar, who drove the events of those years.

E. Badian, *Roman Imperialism in the Late Republic.* Ithaca, NY: Cornell University Press, 1968. This scholarly work discusses Roman expansion in the republic's last two centuries, including the takeover of Macedonia and the conquests of Caesar, whom Badian calls "the greatest brigand of them all." The author's overall theme is that the motivating force behind Roman imperialism, as well as the republic in general, was the superior attitude and greed of the patrician ruling class.

Ernle Bradford, *Julius Caesar: The Pursuit of Power.* New York: William Morrow, 1984. A fine biography of Caesar by a writer known for his penetrating studies of great historical figures, including Hannibal and Christopher Columbus.

James Henry Breasted, *Ancient Times: A History of the Early World.* Boston: Ginn, 1944. Though somewhat dated, this volume remains one of the best general overviews of the ancient world. Well researched, well organized, and clearly written.

J. B. Bury, *The Invasion of Europe by the Barbarians.* New York: W. W. Norton, 1967. A collection of lectures researched and delivered by Bury in the first decade of the twentieth century. Updated and edited, the work remains one of the best all-around discussions of the fifth-century European migrations.

Julius Caesar, *Commentaries on the Gallic Wars*, in *War Commentaries of Caesar*, translated by Rex Warner. New York: New American Library, 1960. A fine translation of Caesar's journals, in which he described in detail his famous military exploits.

Cicero, *Letters to Atticus*, translated by E. O. Winstedt. Cambridge, MA: Harvard University Press, 1961. In these letters covering the last few years of his life, the great champion of the republic commented on Roman politics, Caesar and his murderers, and his own dislike of Cleopatra.

Leonard Cottrell, *A Guide to Roman Britain.* New York: Chilton Books, 1966. Cottrell, a well-known writer about ancient times, offers this useful guidebook to Roman archaeological sites and artifacts in the British Isles. Descriptions of Caesar's and Claudius's invasions and their later effects on Britain are included.

F. R. Cowell, *Cicero and the Roman Republic.* Baltimore: Penguin, 1967. A detailed, scholarly, and very interesting analysis of the Roman Republic, with much background material about Roman customs, as well as a thorough discussion of late republican politics based largely on Cicero's surviving letters.

Donald R. Dudley, *The Romans, 850 B.C.–A.D. 337.* New York: Knopf, 1970.

A thoughtful overview of Roman history and culture. Advanced reading.

Guglielmo Ferrero, *Characters and Events of Roman History, from Caesar to Nero*, translated by Frances L. Ferrero. New York: G. P. Putnam's Sons, 1909. Though dated in some ways, this collection of lectures by the great Italian historian is still a valuable resource. Of main interest here is his "The Development of Gaul," an excellent discussion of how the Romans, particularly Augustus, introduced new culture and industries into Gaul. Advanced reading.

J. F. C. Fuller, *Julius Caesar: Man, Soldier, and Tyrant*. New Brunswick, NJ: Rutgers University Press, 1965. Fuller, a noted military historian, delivers a well-written and thorough biography of Caesar, with plenty of emphasis on the organization of his armies. Advanced reading that will appeal mainly to scholars.

Michael Grant, *Caesar*. London: Weidenfeld and Nicolson, 1974. A fine, easy-to-read general biography by one of the most productive and respected chroniclers of classical civilization. I strongly recommend these other related books by Grant: *The World of Rome*, New American Library, 1960; *The Founders of the Western World: A History of Greece and Rome*, Charles Scribner's Sons, 1991; and especially *The Army of the Caesars*, M. Evans and Company, 1974, which contains much useful and fascinating information about how Caesar and other Roman commanders organized their armies.

John Hackett, ed., *Warfare in the Ancient World*. New York: Facts On File, 1989. An excellent analysis of the weapons, siege devices, and military customs and strategies of the major ancient cultures. Each culture is covered by a noted historian. Among the contributors: Peter Connolly, John Lazenby, and Lawrence Keppie. Highly recommended.

Archer Jones, *The Art of War in the Western World*. New York: Oxford University Press, 1987. A thorough study of evolving military weapons, strategies, ideas, and inventions, and the important figures who introduced them. Contains a lengthy and useful discussion of Caesar's overall Gallic strategy.

Anthony King, *Roman Gaul and Germany*. Berkeley: University of California Press, 1990. An excellent, detailed, scholarly discussion of Roman military operations in and subsequent cultural effects on the lands of central and western Europe.

Kenneth O. Morgan, ed., *The Oxford Illustrated History of Britain*. New York: Oxford University Press, 1986. A fine collection of articles on British history, one of them a comprehensive fifty-one-page summary of Roman Britain by historian Peter Salway.

Plutarch, *Lives of the Noble Grecians and Romans*, excerpted in *Plutarch: Fall of the Roman Republic*, translated by Rex Warner. Baltimore: Penguin Books, 1958. This fine, readable translation of Plutarch includes his biographies of Marius, Sulla, Crassus, Pompey, Caesar, and Cicero. The biography of Marius describes that general's fights against Germanic tribes in Gaul, a prelude to Caesar's later invasion of the region, and the Caesar biography describes Caesar's own exploits in Gaul. Many of the sources Plutarch used have not survived, so his works preserve much knowledge that would otherwise be lost.

Michael Simkins, *Warriors of Rome: An Illustrated History of the Roman Legions.* London: Blandford, 1988. This well-researched work covers major Roman military operations in Gaul, Britain, and other locales. Contains numerous beautiful and accurate paintings of Roman legionnaires doing what they did best—killing, riding, guarding, marching, and intimidating.

Suetonius, *Lives of the Twelve Caesars*, translated by J. C. Rolfe. Cambridge, MA: Harvard University Press, 1964. Besides Plutarch's famous biography of Caesar, this is perhaps the most detailed ancient description of the great general and his exploits.

Lily Ross Taylor, *Party Politics in the Age of Caesar.* Berkeley: University of California Press, 1968. Taylor offers a detailed and thoughtful discussion of the men and institutions of the Roman government in the republic's last years. Includes plenty of material on the dealings and double-dealings of the *populares, optimates,* Cicero, Pompey, Crassus, and, of course, Caesar.

Charles Van Doren, *A History of Knowledge: The Pivotal Events, People, and Achievements of World History.* New York: Ballantine Books, 1991. This informative and extremely well-written book explores what the various early civilizations knew about themselves and their world and how they were affected by new knowledge and inventions. Contains a lucid discussion of the barbarian invasions and how they affected Gaul and other parts of Europe.

Index

on Narbonese conquest, 26
Sulla, Cornelius, 21-22
supplies
    military importance of, 28, 40
    'scorched earth' policy and, 64-65
Switzerland, 13, 30

testudo, 66
Thames River, 53, 54
Tiber River, 15
trireme, 45
Triumvirate, First, 8
    alliance of rivals, 23
    dissolves, 74
    meets at Luca, 43
    overrides Senate, 24, 44
triumvirs (Caesar, Crassus, Pompey), 23, 44

Vallaunodunum, 65

Vandals, 80
Veneti, 44-47
Vercingetorix (Arverni chieftain)
    as powerful leader, 63
    defeated by over-confidence, 68-71
    once in Caesar's cavalry, 62-63
    'scorched earth' tactic and, 64-66, 68
Vistula River, 83

warriors
    British, 34 45, 51, 54
    Etruscan, 16
    Gallic, 11, 17-18, 67, 70
        horsemen, 30, 33
    German
        Suebi, 36, 38
    Helvetian, 33, 34
    Nervii, 41-43
weapons

British, 34, 45
    chariots as, 54
    slashing swords, 79
Celtic, 15
Gallic, 59, 68
    arrows, 66, 69
    invention/imitation of, 59, 67, 68
    lassos, 67
    long swords, 17
    shields, 34
Roman, 10
    hooks (to destroy sails), 46
    secret, 54
    shields, 66
    short swords, 34, 79
    spears, 39, 67, 70, 79
    two-foot swords, 39, 51, 70
    see also siege

Credits

Cover photo: Peter Newark's Historical Pictures

Alinari/Art Resource, NY, 11, 35, 41

Archive Photos, 45

The Bettmann Archive, 10, 16, 19, 39

Culver Pictures, Inc., 18, 23, 38, 53, 58, 62

Hulton Deutsch Collection Limited, 34, 37, 46, 52, 55, 57

Library of Congress, 28, 78

North Wind Picture Archives, 15, 17, 21, 32, 75, 76, 81, 82

Peter Newark's Historical Pictures, 30, 49, 56, 61, 66, 71, 72

The Ny Carlsberg Glyptotek, Copenhagen, 29

Stock Montage, Inc., 67, 69

Grateful acknowledgment is made to reprint excerpts from *The War Commentaries of Caesar*, translated by Rex Warner (a Mentor Book), translation © 1960 by Rex Warner. Reprinted by permission of The New American Library, a division of Penguin Books USA, Inc.

About the Author

Don Nardo is an award-winning author whose more than sixty books cover a wide range of topics. His titles in the Lucent Encyclopedia of Discovery and Invention series alone include: *Lasers, Gravity, Germs, Vaccines, Animation, Computers,* and *Dinosaurs.* A trained historian and history teacher, Mr. Nardo has produced several historical studies, among them *Braving the New World,* the saga of African Americans in colonial times; a political trilogy that includes *Democracy, The U.S. Congress,* and *The U.S. Presidency;* and biographies of Thomas Jefferson, Franklin D. Roosevelt, and Charles Darwin. His specialty is the ancient world, about which he has written *Ancient Greece, The Roman Empire, The Roman Republic, Greek and Roman Theater, The Punic Wars, The Battle of Marathon, The Battle of Zama, Cleopatra,* and what can be considered a companion volume to this discussion of Caesar in Gaul, a detailed biography of Caesar himself. Mr. Nardo has also written numerous screenplays and teleplays, including work for Warner Brothers and ABC Television. He lives with his wife Christine on Cape Cod, Massachusetts.